Curie | Stevens | Hodgkin | Franklin | Roosevelt
Clinton | Parks | Carson | Gandhi
Rankin | Pankhurst | Sanger | de Beauvoir
O'Keeffe | Mother Teresa | Keller | Winfrey

Women who Changed the World

THE MOST REMARKABLE WOMEN
OF THE LAST 100 YEARS

Frank | Steinem | Hepburn | Bhutto
Yousafzai | Morrison | Obama | Thatcher
Perón | Kahlo | Hopper | du Maurier
Merkel | Emin | Yalow | Chanel | Earhart

An Hachette UK Company
www.hachette.co.uk

Published in Great Britain in 2018 by Pyramid,
an imprint of Octopus Publishing Group Ltd
Carmelite House, 50 Victoria Embankment, London EC4Y 0DZ
www.octopusbooks.co.uk

ISBN 978-0-7537-3319-6

A CIP catalogue record for this book is available from the British Library

Printed and bound in China

10 9 8 7 6 5 4 3 2

Publisher: Lucy Pessell
Designer: Lisa Layton
Editor: Sarah Vaughan
Contributing Editor: Emma Hill
Production Controller: Katie Jarvis

Some of this material was previously published in *Defining Moments in Art*, *Defining Moments in Books*,
Defining Moments in History and *Defining Moments in Science*.

Women who Changed the World

THE MOST REMARKABLE WOMEN
OF THE LAST 100 YEARS

CONTENTS

HUMANITY AND LIBERTY

Emmeline Pankhurst

Mother Teresa

Rosa Parks

Eva Perón

Anne Frank

Gloria Steinem

Malala Yousafzai

EMMELINE PANKHURST

JULY 15, 1858–JUNE 14, 1928

BRITISH

Emmeline Pankhurst was a political activist who founded the Women's Franchise League. Famous for being the leader of the British suffragette movement, she helped women win the right to vote.

Emmeline Pankhurst's life was one that began with radical politics. Growing up in Manchester, her parents had their fair share of political involvements – her mother from the Isle of Man, counted amongst generations of women charged with social unrest, and her father having once welcomed American slave abolitionist Henry Ward Beecher upon his visit to Manchester. It was this influence, plus her avid consumption of books and magazines – including the *Women's Suffrage Journal* – that made her "a conscious and confirmed suffragist."

In 1878, Emmeline met her future husband, Richard Pankhurst, a barrister who had for many years advocated for a wealth of liberal causes – such as the freedom of speech and education reform. His understanding of Emmeline's views gave her freedom to break from the traditional role of solely bringing up their children, to involve herself in the Women's Suffrage Society and the Women's Franchise League, before the more militant Women's Social and Political Union (WSPU) in 1903.

The Women's Social and Political Union stood, and protested, for many issues, but the main focus on their agenda was, of course, succeeding in women's right to vote. Along with the active support of her daughters, hunger strikes and arson came to be some of the few violent forms of protest Pankhurst and the WSPU used to gain attention as the newly christened "suffragettes." However, it was upon the beginning of World War I, that the decision was made to cease violence in order to support the war effort, until the demise of the WSPU in 1918, when the Representation of the People Act gave voting rights to all men over the age of 21 and to women over 30.

Following this, and in the later years of her life, Pankhurst's health deteriorated until her death in 1928, shortly before women were granted equal voting rights with men (over the age of 21). Her legacy is one of female empowerment and steadfastness, recently honored by the announcement of a statue to be erected in her home city of Manchester, in 2019.

MOTHER TERESA

AUGUST 26, 1910–SEPTEMBER 5, 1997

ALBANIAN-INDIAN

Known in the Catholic Church as Saint Teresa of Calcutta, her "call" from God resulted in the creation of a great humanitarian leader.

Thirty-six-year-old Sister Teresa was sitting in her seat aboard a train traveling from Calcutta to Darjeeling, on her way to her annual spiritual retreat when, "in a quiet, intimate prayer with our Lord, I heard distinctly, a call within a call. The message was quite clear: I was to leave the convent and help the poor whilst living among them. It was an order."

The former Agnes Gonxha Bojaxhiu of Skopje had long been guided by her faith. In September 1928, she left her family in Macedonia to join the Sisters of Our Lady of Loreto, and took the name Teresa in honor of Saint Teresa of Lisieux, patron saint of missionaries. In 1929, she traveled to Calcutta, where she took her final vows in May 1937.

For nineteen years, she was a beloved teacher and principal at St Mary's School for Girls, but, in 1948, she left her order to follow the Lord's call, calling her departure "my greatest sacrifice." By 1950, she was running her ministry in the slums of Calcutta, known as the Missionaries of Charity.

For the next forty-seven years, Mother Teresa helped feed and comfort the poor, the sick, and the dying, and building an order of more than 5,000 people who fed more than 500,000 families worldwide each year. She died on September 5, 1997, just five days short of the fifty-first anniversary of her "call within a call," a day now celebrated by her order as "Inspiration Day."

ROSA PARKS

FEBRUARY 4, 1913–OCTOBER 25, 2005

AMERICAN

Rosa Parks was a civil-rights activist most famous
for her bus protest, refusing to give up her seat
in the "colored section", when the "white only
section" became full. Parks's subsequent arrest
provided the catalyst to launch the Montgomery
Bus Boycott, which lasted from
1955 to 1956.

On December 1, 1955, Rosa Parks was catapulted into the spotlight as African-Americans mobilized under the leadership of Dr. Martin Luther King Jr. to force Montgomery, Alabama, to revise their policy that allowed white bus riders to sit in the front while African-Americans were relegated to the back of the bus, even when the first ten seats were empty.

After a long day of work as a seamstress, Mrs Parks boarded a bus and sat down in the section reserved for whites only. Late in the afternoon, during peak time for people leaving work, the bus began to fill and when a white man entered, she refused to move. The bus driver alerted police, who promptly arrested Parks and fingerprinted her.

The eyes of the country were thrust on the dignified, soft-spoken woman, whereupon civil-rights leaders used her case to spotlight the racial injustice of Montgomery's bus system. The boycott lasted well into the middle of 1956, when the Federal Court ruled it was unconstitutional to have separate seating for African-Americans on city buses.

This marked a significant victory for the civil-rights movement, but Mrs Parks's name and face had become synonymous with the boycott in Alabama and across the country. Unable to obtain work, she and her family left Montgomery with the satisfaction that her courageous act provided the civil-rights movement with the energy needed to push for the equality of all citizens of the United States.

EVA PERÓN

MAY 7, 1919–JULY 26, 1952

ARGENTINIAN

Eva Perón, First Lady of Argentina, became
a legendary political figure through her
impassioned fight for the rights of women and to
improve the lives of the poor in her country.

Perón was born in the small town of Los Toldos on the Argentine Pampas. Her parents, Juan Duarte and Juana Ibarguren, were not married, and her father had another wife and family. Perón and her siblings grew up in poverty, a situation that only worsened following her father's death in 1926. When Eva was 15, she travelled to Buenos Aires to pursue her dream of becoming an actress, and eventually began performing in radio plays. Then, around the age of 20, she started her own radio production business, the Company of the Theater of the Air.

Eva's life was set to change dramatically in 1945 when she married government official and colonel, Juan Perón. The following year, he became president and Perón's career as First Lady began. She was adored by her people and wielded great political influence. She acted as de facto Minister of Health and Minister of Labor, awarding generous wage increases to the unions, who responded with political support for Perón. She made many enemies among the political elite after cutting off government subsidies to the traditional Sociedad de Beneficencia, replacing it with the Eva Peron Foundation, supported by lottery funding and voluntary contributions from unions and businesses. She used this to establish thousands of charitable organisations, including hospitals, orphanages, schools, and homes for the elderly.

Always her aim was to help people in poverty lead better lives. Eva formed the Peronista Feminist Party in 1949, and fought for women's suffrage. In 1951, in spite of the fact that she was dying from cancer, she obtained the nomination for vice president, but was forced by the army to withdraw her candidacy.

Even after her death, Perón remained a potent political figure, inspiring her followers to attempt to have her canonized and her enemies to steal her embalmed body and take it to Italy in an attempt to eradicate her legacy as a national symbol.

ANNE FRANK

JUNE 12, 1929–MARCH, 1945

GERMAN

The posthumous publication of Anne Frank's diary, *The Diary of a Young Girl* provided the world with a face for the 1.5 million Jewish children murdered in the Holocaust, and became one of the most distinct 20th-century literary achievements. For future generations, her diary is a key to remembering the genocide as well as to honoring the dead, and her unmitigated faith in humanity is an inspiration.

The world knew about the atrocities of the Holocaust long before the end of World War II, but the legacy of Anne Frank provided an individualist sense of tragedy to the genocidal events. A German-Jewish teenager whose family hid in Nazi-occupied Holland before getting shipped off to concentration camps, Frank kept a candid diary that combined the standard observations of a 15-year-old girl with the harsh reality of oppressive times.

First published in the Netherlands in 1947, under the title *Het Achterhuis*, or *The Secret Annexe*, Anne's diary expresses the frustration of confinement and the fear of being discovered, while chronicling the shifting emotions of any girl passing from childhood to adolescence, rebelling against her parents, and falling in love.

While Anne Frank died of typhus at the Bergen-Belsen concentration camp in 1945, her father, Otto, survived the war and discovered her personal musings. Frank's transcription of the diary caught the attention of a historian and landed a mention in the newspaper *Het Parool*. A publication deal followed in 1947, and its English translation in 1951 brought the phenomenon of *The Diary of a Young Girl* into full swing. A Broadway play entitled *The Diary of Anne Frank* opened in 1955, while there's a 1959 film of the same name. In 1960 the Anne Frank House in Amsterdam was turned into a museum, and became one of the city's most popular tourist attractions.

Over the years, Anne Frank's story has captivated readers (and audiences of its film and stage adaptations) due to the startlingly insightful perspective of its young protagonist. While Frank mused on typical family issues, her existentially poignant scrutinizing of the Nazi occupation put a human face on the massacre. "It's a wonder I haven't abandoned all my ideals," she wrote. "Yet I cling to them because I still believe, in spite of everything, that people are truly good at heart."

❦

GLORIA STEINEM

MARCH 25, 1934

AMERICAN

A social activist, writer, editor, lecturer, and feminist organizer, Gloria Steinem has been at the forefront of the women's-rights movement since the late 1960s, campaigning passionately for social justice ever since.

Steinem was born in Toledo, Ohio, and spent her early childhood traveling with her parents in a house trailer. From a young age, it was clear that Steinem would not follow the traditional path expected of a woman at that time – settling down to marriage and having a family was not on her agenda. Instead, she studied government at Smith College, Massachusetts, and, after completing her degree in 1956, received a fellowship to study in India. Her time there ignited an interest in grassroots activism that would later inspire her work in the field of women's liberation and the Equal Rights Amendment.

On her return to the U.S., Steinem carved out a career for herself as a freelance writer and became increasingly involved in the women's-rights movement, leading marches, and touring the country as a speaker, where she found herself very much in demand.

In 1971, she founded the National Women's Political Caucus (NWPC) with Betty Friedan, Bella Abzug, and Shirley Chisholm, which continues today to promote gender equality and ensure the election of more women to public office. She went on to launch the trailblazing *Ms* magazine, which dealt with contemporary issues from a feminist perspective and was not afraid to tackle difficult subjects such as domestic violence.

An acclaimed journalist and award-winning writer, Steinem has written extensively on women's issues, with books and essays that have always garnered attention and sometimes controversy. Steinem was awarded the Presidential Medal of Freedom in 2013 and was an honorary co-chair and speaker at the Women's March on Washington in 2017, the day after the inauguration of Donald Trump as President. Her words continue to empower and inspire.

MALALA YOUSAFZAI

JULY 12, 1997

PAKISTANI

Activist Malala Yousafzai defied the Taliban in Pakistan by demanding that girls should be able to receive an education and attracted global attention when she survived an assassination attempt at the age of just 15.

In 2007, the Swat Valley, where Yousafzai was born, was invaded by the Taliban and strict Islamic laws were imposed on its inhabitants. The girls' schools were shut down or destroyed and women were forbidden to take any active role in society.

In 2008, at the age of 11, Yousafzai went with her social-activist father to a press club in Peshawar and it's here that she gave her first impassioned speech, "How Dare the Taliban Take Away My Basic Right to Education?", which was publicized throughout the country. Soon after, the BBC contacted Yousafzai's father. They were looking for someone to blog about life under Taliban rule, so Yousafzai wrote anonymously about her daily life for BBC Urdu.

Television appearances and coverage in the international media followed. She was identified as the BBC's blogger and achieved widespread acclaim for her courageous activism. In 2011, Yousafzai was nominated by Desmond Tutu for the International Children's Peace Prize and was awarded Pakistan's first National Youth Peace Prize (later renamed the National Malala Peace Prize).

In 2012, Yousafzai was shot in the head by a Taliban gunman on her way home from school. She survived the attack and was flown to England for surgery. Here she returned to her studies and her activism, undeterred by the violence that nearly ended her life. In 2013, Yousafzai won the United Nations Human Rights Prize and was named one of *Time* magazine's most-influential people and, in the following year, she became the youngest recipient of the Nobel Peace Prize. She is the author of *I Am Malala*, and now uses her profile to highlight human-rights issues around the world, funding projects through the Malala Fund, which was set up in her name.

❦

SCIENCE

Nettie Stevens

Marie Curie

Lise Meitner

Inge Lehmann

Barbara McClintock

Maria Goeppert Mayer

Margeurite Perey

Mary Leakey

Katsuko Saruhashi

Rosalind Franklin

Rosalyn Yalow

Martha Chase

NETTIE STEVENS

JULY 7, 1861–MAY 4, 1912

AMERICAN

Nettie Stevens gave rise to the field of genetics by discovering the basis for one of the principal theories in biology – that gender is determined by chromosomes.

Nettie Stevens was one of the first female scientists to make a name for herself in the biological sciences. She was born in the small town of Cavendish, Vermont. Despite the grim educational opportunities for women at this time, Stevens excelled in mathematics and science. She attended a teachers' college and taught for a number of years before she decided to further her own education.

Stevens earned a Master's degree in biology in 1900, and moved to Bryn Mawr College in Pennsylvania, where she studied under Thomas Hunt Morgan. After receiving her Ph.D., and a glowing recommendation from Morgan, in 1903, she moved to the Carnegie Institute of Washington, to perform original research on sex determination.

Initially working on mealworms, Stevens showed, in 1905, that when an egg was fertilized with a sperm containing an X chromosome, it became a female; with a Y chromosome sperm, it became a male. This simple explanation was the basis of sex determination. Coincidentally, a former Bryn Mawr researcher, Edmund Beecher Wilson, published a very similar paper the same year and their discovery provided the first clear link between a heritable characteristic and a specific chromosome.

Sadly, Stevens died from breast cancer in 1912, unable to occupy a professorship back at Bryn Mawr which had been created especially for her.

❦

MARIE CURIE

NOVEMBER 7, 1867–JULY 4, 1934

FRENCH-POLISH

Marie Curie is sometimes known as the "Mother of Modern Physics," and it was she who coined the word "radioactivity" through her invaluable research in the field.

Marie Curie (née Maria Skłodowska) was born in Poland in 1867, and is famous for her work in the investigation of radioactivity and her pioneering status as an acknowledged female scientist. Outstandingly intelligent, she studied physics and mathematics at the Sorbonne (University of Paris), and graduated with a degree in physics and, a year later, a second degree in math.

In 1895, she married Pierre Curie, and together they explored radioactive emissions from certain elements, building on the work of Henri Becquerel and his discovery of radioactivity in uranium. Their research led them to the source of radiation, and they were able to demonstrate that radioactivity is an atomic property, rather than a property of interaction between elements. They subsequently discovered polonium and radium, and Marie's work on the isolation of radium earned her the first science doctorate to be awarded to a woman in Europe. In 1903, she was awarded, along with her husband and Becquerel, the Nobel Prize for Physics.

Tragically, Pierre Curie was killed in a street accident in 1906, and Marie, and her daughters, were devastated. But her work ethic and mental toughness saw her through. She continued her research and took on Pierre's teaching job, becoming, in yet another "first" for feminism, the first woman to teach at the Sorbonne. Her *Treatise on Radioactivity*, published in 1910, was an explanation of her research on radioactivity, and helped earn her the Nobel Prize for Chemistry the following year.

She later worked on medical applications for radium with her daughter, Irene. Due to her constant exposure to radiation before the dangers were known, Marie Curie developed aplastic anemia in the 1920s, and died on July 4, 1934.

LISE MEITNER

NOVEMBER 7, 1878–OCTOBER 27, 1968

AUSTRIAN-SWEDISH

A physicist who specialized in nuclear physics and radioactivity, her discovery – with a small group of scientists – of nuclear fission, led to the development of the atomic bomb and nuclear energy.

Just a year before World War II erupted in Europe, Otto Hahn was working on an experiment with Lise Meitner in Germany. They were trying to create elements with heavier atoms than could be found in nature, by firing neutrons at uranium in the hope that they would stick. In the middle of the experiment, Hitler's purges forced Meitner, who was Jewish, to flee to Sweden.

When Hahn came to analyze the results on his own, he found that, far from producing heavier elements they had produced lighter ones – radium and barium. Hahn was puzzled; radium is only a little lighter, but barium has exactly half the atomic mass of uranium. Creating these much lighter atoms would require the neutron to knock around a hundred particles out of the nucleus of uranium, which seemed impossible. Baffled, Hahn sent the results to Meitner.

Meitner discussed the puzzling results with her nephew, physicist Otto Frisch. It didn't take them long to work out what was happening. When a neutron was fired at a uranium atom, it was absorbed by the nucleus, making the atom unstable. The easiest way for the atom to become stable again was to split in half, creating two barium atoms. These two atoms had less mass in total than a single uranium atom – the lost mass was converted into energy as described by Albert Einstein's famous equation, $E=mc^2$.

Inadvertently, their experiment had set the wheels in motion for the production of the atomic bomb, and changed the face of war for ever.

❦

INGE LEHMANN

MAY 13, 1888–FEBRUARY 21, 1993

DANISH

Inge Lehmann bettered our understanding of Earth's interior, which was necessary for learning more about its formation and the internal processes that govern its evolution.

Traveling to the Earth's core is somewhat problematic. The distance and amount of tunneling involved is one thing, but it's the crushing pressures and sweltering temperatures that really put it out of the question. So how on Earth did Inge Lehmann, a Danish scientist, discover in 1936 that the planet's center comprises a solid inner core surrounded by a molten liquid outer core? The answer is: she studied waves.

After studying mathematics at the University of Copenhagen, and briefly at the University of Cambridge, Lehmann returned to the University of Copenhagen as an assistant in which time she studied seismology, resulting in her being awarded with a degree in 1928. This lead to her becoming head of the department of seismology at the Geodetical Institute of Denmark, the beginning of her key findings in this field.

Seismic waves, generated by earthquakes and explosions, ripple through Earth, and can be measured and recorded using the aptly named seismograph, invented in 1880. There are two particular kinds of wave that seismologists depend on in order to understand the internal structure of Earth: P (primary) waves, which can penetrate fluids and solids; and S (secondary) waves, which can only pass through solids. Both types bend or reflect, and change speed as they travel, indicating that Earth's interior consists of layers with different densities, both liquid and solid.

Before Lehmann's discovery, seismologists had proposed a molten liquid core, encompassed by a solid mantle and an outer thin crust, all separated by density changes called discontinuities. But when Lehmann studied the shock waves of an earthquake in New Zealand in 1929, she noticed weak P-waves being detected in areas of Europe, which the liquid core theory couldn't explain. She hypothesized that Earth must have a solid inner core with an outer liquid core, separated by what is now called the Lehmann discontinuity.

BARBARA MCCLINTOCK

JUNE 16, 1902–SEPTEMBER 2, 1992

AMERICAN

Barbara McClintock's discovery of jumping genes led to great advances in genetic engineering, and earned her the Nobel Prize for Physiology or Medicine in 1983.

You may have seen "wild maize" used as a centerpiece for a meal; it stands out from the bland yellow maize by having red, brown, and even blue kernels. The colors come from pigments in the endosperm – the tasty bit of the corn which stores nutrients for the seed. Each ear of maize is formed by multiple flowers, and if the flowers are fertilized by sperm carrying different genes for endosperm pigment, different color kernels will arise. If you look closely at a colored kernel, you might see even more variation: blue among red; purple against brown.

Barbara McClintock was an American scientist and cytogeneticist who started her lifelong career as the leader in the development of maize cytogenetics, looking very closely at them and seeing discordance: multiple colors that could not be explained by Mendel's laws of inheritance. McClintock suspected that the variegation was caused by instability of the genes that coded for the pigment.

She eventually identified the series of genes that determine pigmentation, located on chromosome number 9. Changes in the kernels' color occurred when a small piece of chromosome 9 moved from one place to another, close to a gene coding for a pigment, turning it off. McClintock called these sections of genetic material "control elements."

These are now more commonly referred to as "jumping genes" or transposons, which many other organisms have. They are responsible for much of the antibiotic resistance of bacteria; enable certain parasites to evade their host's immune system; and some even lead to cancers. Recognised as one of the best in this field of study, McClintock was awarded many fellowships and elected a member of the National Academy of Sciences in 1944.

MARIA
GOEPPERT MAYER

JUNE 28, 1906–FEBRUARY 20, 1972

AMERICAN-GERMAN

Maria Goeppert Mayer developed a new model
of the atom and was one of the great pioneers for
women in scientific research.

Maria Goeppert Mayer was never going to be an underachiever. Born into a family of seven generations of university professors, her academic prowess would have come as no great surprise. But she surpassed all expectations, contributing greatly to the field of nuclear physics and bagging a Nobel Prize to boot.

Goeppert Mayer began her university studies in physics at a time when quantum mechanics was new and exciting. Although her academic career was interrupted by the Depression during the 1930s, which limited her research posts, she made many important contributions to the emerging field, despite often having to work for no money. In 1946, with only very limited knowledge of the area, she began working on a model of the atom.

The Nobel Prize she received in 1963 was for her discovery and application of this model, which described how protons and neutrons are arranged into shells within the nucleus. They had previously been thought to be randomly colliding, but Goeppert Mayer showed that discrete energy states existed. Her work also showed why isotopes of elements – forms of elements that have different numbers of neutrons in the nucleus – are less stable.

Goeppert Mayer's career is remembered yearly in the form of an award to a female scientist or engineer at an early stage in her career. Mayer often encouraged women to engage in scientific careers and follow in her distinguished scientific footsteps.

MARGUERITE PEREY

OCTOBER 19, 1909–MAY 13, 1975

FRENCH

A student of physicist Marie Curie, Perey's discovery of francium filled a gap in the Periodic Table, and refined our knowledge of the atom.

Francium isn't the most famous of elements. Indeed, after astatine it's the second scarcest in nature. Little wonder then, that its discovery took until the eve of World War II, making it the last of the natural elements to be found.

The radioactive species was finally isolated in France (hence the name), in 1939, by Marguerite Perey. She'd taken a technician's position as Marie Curie's personal assistant in 1929, and soon became an expert on the little understood element actinium. It was while attempting to find the half-life of this element that she made her discovery. A highly pure sample of actinium-227 showed an unexpectedly rapid decay to a particle that behaved chemically like an alkali metal.

Perey had spotted the long sought-after element, which had been missing from the foot of Group I on the Periodic Table. After some internal squabbling among her superiors, she was given full credit for the discovery. The element – the 87th in the table – was given its official name in 1949. Because it is rare and unstable, francium is a useless element as far as practical applications go. Instead, it pulls its weight in the laboratory.

Francium has a relatively simple atomic structure, making it a useful testbed for probing electron energy levels. Our understanding of atomic structure and interactions has been much improved thanks to this Gallic latecomer from Perey.

MARY LEAKEY

FEBRUARY 6 ,1913–DECEMBER 9, 1996

BRITISH

Mary Leakey, FBA, was a paleoanthropologist who was the first person to discover a Proconsul skull and footprints to show our ancestors had walked upright. She and her team gave scientists a first glimpse of the timescales of this evolutionary stage.

In 1978, Mary Leakey and her team came across what was to become one of the most important set of footprints ever found. They belonged to two individuals, who walked over the wet volcanic ash at a site in Laetoli, Tanzania, some 3.5 million years before. For the first time, the footprints showed that human ancestors known as Australopithecus had walked upright using a perfect two-footed stride, with no knuckle imprints that would have suggested the use of all fours.

Before this discovery, we had no time scale for when human ancestors might have gone from getting around on four legs to walking on two. The prints showed the characteristically human arch in the foot and didn't have the same large big toe that other apes have. The footprints were not damaged because they had been covered in powdery ash. This was then cemented by soft rain, making a perfect imprint that would not be destroyed over millions of years.

Information from the footprint size and the length of pace suggested that the two hominids would have been about 1.34–1.56 meters tall and 1.15–1.34 meters tall respectively. The Laetoli site is located just 45 kilometers from another famous archaeological site, Olduvai Gorge, where many human tools and skeletons have been found over the years including those of *Homo habilis*.

Mary Leakey, along with her husband, Louis, and son, Richard, carried out significant research in the field of archaeology.

KATSUKO SARUHASHI

MARCH 22, 1920–SEPTEMBER 29, 2007

JAPANESE

Pioneering geochemist Katsuko Saruhashi's work helped to prove how nuclear fallout spreads through the oceans. As well as making groundbreaking discoveries, she also nurtured the careers of other women and inspired them to work and flourish in the field of science.

Tokyo-born Saruhashi became the first woman to earn a doctorate in chemistry from the University of Tokyo, where she was also the first person to accurately measure carbonic acid concentration levels based on pH level, chlorine concentration and temperature. In a life of "firsts," she went on to become the first woman to be elected to the Science Council of Japan (in 1980) and the first woman to win the Miyake Prize for geochemistry (in 1985).

Saruhashi's carbonic-acid measurement technique, named Saruhashi's Table, became critical to oceanographers around the globe and her work proved that fallout from the U.S. atomic tests that took place in the 50s on the Marshall Islands reached Japan less than two years later. Her research on how nuclear fallout spreads through seawater has been credited with helping to persuade the Soviet Union and the United States to halt nuclear testing.

Saruhashi's scientific achievements are vast, but her work in empowering female scientists in her wake is just as impressive. In 1958, she established the Society of Japanese Women Scientists to promote women in the field of science and in 1981 she founded the Saruhashi Prize, awarded annually to outstanding Japanese women researchers.

She was passionate about gender equality long before it was commonplace to be so, once declaring, "I would like to see the day when women can contribute to science and technology on an equal footing with men."

ROSALIND FRANKLIN

JULY 25, 1920–APRIL 16, 1958

ENGLISH

Rosalind Franklin's work as a chemist and X-ray crystallographer facilitated the discovery of the molecular structure of DNA.

The scientists traditionally credited with uncovering the structure of DNA are James Watson, Francis Crick, and Maurice Wilkins. But traditional accounts of their discovery fail to acknowledge the contributions of one brilliant individual – Rosalind Franklin. It is now generally accepted that the role played by her was substantial.

Having spent several years in France using X-rays to make images of biological molecules, Franklin had arrived in London in 1950 to begin work on DNA. But her skilful X-ray imagery, observations, and conclusions were trivialized – due to what might be termed a clash of personalities – by James Watson in his personal account of the discovery of DNA, *The Double Helix*. One of Franklin's images, "photo 51," was shown to Watson and Crick without Franklin's knowledge. It showed an X-shaped diffraction pattern, suggesting that overlapping helical structures made up DNA. James Watson saw the image and felt a key question had been answered.

In his version, Franklin was presented as a subordinate of Wilkins at King's College. This myth persisted for some time. In fact, it was the communication of Franklin's data and conclusions to Watson and Crick by Maurice Wilkins and Max Perutz that revealed missing pieces of the puzzle. These, along with data from other sources, allowed them to assemble their full description of DNA structure. Their model appeared in the journal *Nature* in April, 1953. Franklin was not informed about the publication, despite the fact that it was her photograph that had for the first time revealed the iconic double helix.

Rosalind Franklin died from cancer at the age of thirty-seven, and has since been verbally credited by Watson and Crick for her contribution. In 1962, Crick, Watson, and Wilkins were awarded the Nobel Prize in Physiology or Medicine – a prize that is not traditionally awarded posthumously.

ROSALYN YALOW

JULY 19, 1921–MAY 30, 2011

AMERICAN

Rosalyn Yalow flourished in a male-dominated field, with no formal medical education, and – in the radioimmunoassay (RIA) technique – gave the world of medicine a gold-standard tool for clinical analysis.

Born in New York, in 1921, Rosalyn Yalow was a determined academic, excelling at a time when expectations of women were not high. She was brilliant in mathematics and chemistry, but it was physics that piqued her interest during the 1930s. Her future was decided when she sat through a lecture about nuclear fission.

She started teaching at the University of Illinois in 1941, and was the only woman in a four-hundred-strong faculty. She worked throughout the war and obtained her Ph.D. in 1945, an expert in the measurement of radioactive substances. Back in New York, her husband introduced her to medical physics, an ideal platform for her knowledge.

Yalow first developed a major radioisotope service and then began to research the clinical applications of radioisotopes. While working on insulin, the idea of antibodies as a measuring tool occurred to her. It took several more years to develop the radioimmunoassay, but in 1959 the technology was finally launched.

Now found in laboratories worldwide, the radioimmunoassay measures with extraordinary sensitivity hundreds of chemical substances in body fluids, using antibodies and radioactive "labels." It has countless uses, from screening donated blood for contaminants to identifying drug abusers. Remarkably, Yalow had no formal medical training despite this massive contribution to medicine. She was awarded the Nobel Prize for Physiology or Medicine in 1977, for the technique she had devised with her colleague Solomon Berson nearly twenty years earlier.

MARTHA CHASE

NOVEMBER 30, 1927–AUGUST 8, 2003

AMERICAN

An American geneticist who helped confirm
that DNA, not protein, is the genetic material
of life, responsible for passing on all
hereditary information.

DNA was first isolated in 1869 by Friedrich Miescher, but its exact function remained elusive for a number of years, until a series of experiments with viruses and bacteria showed that it was in fact the hereditary material of all life forms.

Bacteriophages are viruses that are able to invade and inject their DNA into bacteria, effectively taking them hostage. Originally, it was thought that the outer protein "coat" of a bacteriophage was the material that passed between the two, but the American biologists Alfred Hershey and Martha Chase proved this theory wrong.

Hershey and Chase exploited the infection cycle of a virus known as T2, to show how DNA is transferred. They labeled viral coats and DNA, by attaching radioactive molecules to them, and allowed them to infect *E. coli* bacteria. The viruses were then separated from the bacteria to look for the labels. They found that radiation marking showed up inside the bacteria when the DNA had been labeled, suggesting the viruses were causing infection by inserting their DNA.

Offspring of the bacteria also contained radioactive DNA, showing that it could be passed on during replication. We now know these viruses attach to a bacteria cell surface and inject their DNA inside. This initial work – for which Hershey was awarded the 1969 Nobel Prize in Physiology or Medicine – changed what we know about viral infections such as flu and the common cold, and this crucial information shared by Hershey and Chase became one of the inspirations for Watson, Wilkins and Crick in solving the mystery of DNA structure.

⚜

MEDICINE

❀

Florence Nightingale

❀

Margaret Sanger

❀

Dorothy Hodgkin

❀

Gertrude Elion

❀

Elizabeth Blackburn

❀

Nancy Wexler

FLORENCE NIGHTINGALE

MAY 12, 1820–AUGUST 13, 1910

ENGLISH

Florence Nightingale, known as "The Lady with the Lamp," was a pioneer of modern nursing, a writer, and a recognized statistician, celebrated for her contribution to nursing in the Crimean War, as well as becoming the first woman to receive the Order of Merit.

Florence Nightingale was named after the Italian city in which she was born on May 12, 1820. As a young woman, she was widely admired, considered highly intelligent, and was thus expected to make a good marriage. But in 1837, Florence had what she described as her "calling" from God. She undertook nurse training in Germany, which led to her appointment as superintendent of the Establishment for Gentlewomen in 1853.

When Britain, France, and Turkey declared war on Russia in 1854, Nightingale arrived at the Barrack Hospital in Scutari, a suburb in Asian Constantinople, with 38 nurses. Although doctors did not instantly welcome the introduction of female nurses to military hospitals, the nurses were soon crucial in attending the continuous arrival of wounded soldiers. In addition to devoted nursing, Nightingale wrote home on behalf of the soldiers, sent their wages to their families, and introduced reading rooms to the hospital.

After the Crimean War, Nightingale became a central figure in the campaign for a Royal Commission to investigate the health of the British Army. She also contributed to Army and hospital statistics, leading her to become the first woman to be elected a fellow of the Royal Statistical Society in 1858. Two years later, she established the Nightingale Training School for nurses at St Thomas' Hospital, and published her best-known work, *Notes on Nursing*. In her final years, Nightingale received many honors, becoming the first woman to receive the Order of Merit, in 1907. She died on August 13, 1910, aged 90.

MARGARET SANGER

SEPTEMBER 14, 1879–SEPTEMBER 6, 1966

AMERICAN

A feminist icon for her activism for birth control, sex education, and nursing, Margaret Sanger's birth-control clinic brought public attention to the fledgling birth-control movement and paved the way for the recognition of the constitutional rights of American women to control their own bodies.

Margaret Sanger, who opened the first birth-control clinic in the United States, is considered one of the most important figures of the twentieth century. As a nurse in New York City, Sanger often saw women from poor families who could not support the children they had year after year, and who died or grew old before their time from repeated pregnancies.

Sanger realized that women would never be free until they could control their reproductive lives; however, most states prohibited the dispensing of birth-control information and devices. After several physicians refused to help establish a birth-control clinic, Sanger launched it with only her sister, Ethel Byrne, and her secretary, Fania Mindell. The clinic opened on October 16, 1916, in a curtained storefront window in Brooklyn, New York. By 5 p.m., 140 women had arrived.

Over the next several days, 464 women sought help. On the tenth day, a well-dressed woman was immediately identified as an undercover policewoman. The next day, the women were arrested, and the clinic was closed.

When American women were given suffrage rights in 1920, Sanger was allowed to operate in a less hostile but still precarious environment. In 1924, she opened the Birth Control Clinical Research Bureau where women were seen by a licensed physician. In 1942, the name was changed to Planned Parenthood Federation of America. Planned Parenthood became an international organization in 1953, and, thanks to Margaret Sanger's efforts, most governments now recognize the importance of women's rights and family planning.

DOROTHY HODGKIN

MAY 12, 1910–JULY 29, 1994

BRITISH

As a chemist who developed protein crystallography, Dorothy Hodgkin's contributions to understanding the structure of natural molecules have led to the development of crucial drugs and saved many lives.

Dorothy Hodgkin, one of the most famous British women scientists, was actually born in Egypt. For thirty-five years of her illustrious career, she worked on the structure of insulin, and improving the technique of X-ray crystallography to enable it to work out the structure of large and complex biological molecules.

The structure of insulin was finally resolved in 1969, but, always conscious of the importance of applying her research to improve humanity, Hodgkin continued to work on insulin and its role in understanding and treating diabetes. Alongside her work on insulin, she used X-ray crystallography to determine the structure of other biologically important molecules such as cholesterol, penicillin, and vitamin B12, which led to the award of the Nobel Prize for Chemistry in 1964.

In 1965, Dame Dorothy followed in the footsteps of Florence Nightingale as only the second woman ever to become a member of the Order of Merit. Hodgkin was heavily influenced by the eminent chemist and social historian, John Desmond Bernal – not just in her research, but also in developing a strong social conscience.

She was an active campaigner for social justice and peace, and was President of the Pugwash Conferences on Science and World Affairs from 1976 to 1988. During this period, she asked all living Nobel scientists to sign a declaration against nuclear weapons; one hundred and eleven of them did so.

GERTRUDE ELION

JANUARY 23, 1918–FEBRUARY 21, 1999

AMERICAN

As a biochemist and pharmacologist, Gertrude
Elion helped create many key medications,
including the first successful anti-leukemia drugs.

In retrospect, Gertrude Elion was an unlikely candidate to have developed some of the most important medicines of the 20th century. Her parents had immigrated to New York City from Eastern Europe in the early 1900s; her father studying dentistry and eventually practicing in their apartment. The stock market crash left the family in dire financial straits, and it was unlikely that young Gertrude would be able to further her education.

Her grades, however, secured her a place at Hunter College, New York, where she chose to study chemistry. After a series of odd jobs, which included teaching chemistry at high-school level, and checking the color of mayonnaise and the acidity of pickles for an industrial food service, she joined George Hitchings's lab in 1944. Elion would later share the 1988 Nobel Prize in Physiology or Medicine with her new boss and Sir James Black for discoveries of "important new principles of drug treatment."

In the 1940s, it was known that in order to reproduce, cells had to incorporate certain substrates to synthesize nucleic acid. Elion and Hitchings realized that if medications that resembled these substrates were incorporated into cells instead, they might halt further synthesis, and could therefore be used to target rogue or diseased cells, preventing them from replicating.

Together they developed drugs to combat leukemia, malaria, gout, and herpes, as well as the anti-rejection medicine azathioprine, which is used to suppress the immune system after a transplant operation.

ELIZABETH BLACKBURN

NOVEMBER 26, 1948

AUSTRALIAN-AMERICAN

An Australian-American Nobel laureate and
former President of the Salk Institute for
Biological Studies, Elizabeth Blackburn discovered
a protein that could explain both how cells age
and how they turn cancerous.

Every chromosome is capped by special structures called telomeres, like the plastic bits on the end of shoelaces. They prevent chromosomes from fraying or fusing together. Today, telomere research is one of the most exciting branches of molecular biology and much of this work was inspired by an Australian-born scientist called Elizabeth Blackburn.

In the 1970s, Blackburn started working on telomeres by studying a single-celled microbe called *Tetrahymena*, whose abundance of telomeres were easier to study than the small number found in human cells. Blackburn soon found that telomeres are actually short, repeated bits of DNA, but her work really took off in 1985, when, together with student Carolyn Greider, she discovered a protein called telomerase that lengthens telomeres.

That discovery formed the basis for future work that linked telomeres to both aging and cancer. Telomerase isn't active in most cells, so their telomeres shorten as they age. This makes the cells' chromosomes more vulnerable, and eventually stops them from dividing (and renewing) altogether. On the other hand, cells with indefinitely active telomerase can rejuvenate their telomeres and are effectively immortal. These include stem cells and, more sinisterly, the vast majority of cancer cells. Several cancer researchers have their sights set on telomerase as a target for future drugs.

Today, Blackburn is contributing heavily to the field she kick-started, not least by inspiring new generations of female scientists. In a typically male-biased field, telomere research is still dominated by women.

NANCY WEXLER

JULY 19, 1945

AMERICAN

Nancy Wexler is an American geneticist best known for her contribution in the discovery of the location of the gene that causes Huntington's disease – a genetic marker allowed families to determine their future potential for the disease, and brought scientists one step closer to a cure.

Huntington's disease is an inherited disease of the central nervous system, usually manifesting itself when a patient is between thirty-five and forty-five years of age. In the early 1980s, there was no predictive test for Huntington's disease. Through the work of American scientists Nancy Wexler and James Gusella, however, a genetic marker was found which allowed the offspring of Huntington's parents to see if they would develop and perhaps pass on the disease.

In 1981, Wexler, a geneticist of Columbia University and the Hereditary Disease Foundation, traveled to a Venezuelan village experiencing an extremely high rate of Huntington's disease. As a daughter of a Huntongton's patient, this was a cause that was very close to her heart. She constructed a family tree of over 3,000 village members, and obtained blood and skin samples from 570 living descendants. Wexler passed these samples on to Gusella at Massachusetts General Hospital, who was working on finding a marker for Huntington's disease.

By using pieces of DNA called probes, Gusella's group tediously examined Wexler's samples and located an area of distinctive DNA on chromosome four. It was thought that if these varying DNA regions frequently corresponded to incidence of disease, then the disease gene was located near this region. This was the first time a disease gene had been mapped to a specific chromosome based on inheritance and genetic markers alone.

This significant scientific achievement allowed families of Huntington's patients to find out if they were also at risk from the disease. With the discovery of the exact mutation sequence in 1993, scientists are now a few steps closer to finding a cure.

TECHNOLOGY

Hertha Ayrton

Amelia Earhart

Grace Hopper

Stephanie Kwolek

HERTHA AYRTON

APRIL 28, 1854–AUGUST 26, 1923

BRITISH

Hertha Ayrton was the first woman invited to read a paper at the Royal Society, the world's oldest scientific academy.

Phoebe Sarah Marks was educated with her cousins, who first introduced her to mathematics and science. She took the Cambridge University examination for women, and from 1877 to 1881 read mathematics at Girton College – co-founded by her friend Barbara Bodichon as a women's college – where she changed her name to Hertha.

Back in London, in 1884, Ayrton attended evening classes on electricity run by William Ayrton, an electrical engineer. His wife, a pioneering woman doctor, had died the previous year, and Ayrton and William were married in 1885. As well as giving lectures to women about electricity and its potential to change their domestic lives, Hertha also took over her husband's experiments on the electric arc, demonstrating a linear relationship between arc length, pressure, and potential difference, known as the Ayrton equation.

Ayrton's analysis, presented in 12 papers in *The Electrician*, established her unique reputation as a brilliant female electrical engineer. She was elected a member of the Institution of Electrical Engineers (IIE), the only female member until 1958. Her lecture to the International Electrical Congress in Paris in 1900 helped persuade the British Association to allow women onto their committees.

Although proposed as a candidate for the Royal Society in 1902, she was ineligible as a married woman with no standing in the law. Yet, in 1904, she became the first woman to read a paper of her own work to the society. Then, in 1906, Ayrton was awarded the society's prestigious Hughes Medal for her scientific work, and is only one of two women recipients to date.

AMELIA EARHART

JULY 24, 1897–JULY 2, 1937

AMERICAN

Despite being the first female aviator to fly solo across the Atlantic Ocean, Amelia Earhart's life is often overshadowed by her mysterious disappearance whilst on a flight.

Had things gone according to schedule, Amelia Earhart would not have been flying across the blue expanse of the Pacific on July 2, 1937. The original plan had envisioned completing the Pacific first, but an accident during takeoff from Pearl Harbor caused a lengthy delay, and the seasonal weather patterns changed.

When Earhart and her navigator, Fred Noonan, took off from California on May 21, they headed east. By June 29, they had crossed North America, Africa, Southeast Asia, and Australia, and reached Lae, Papua New Guinea. Ahead of them lay the most daunting leg of the journey: the 2,566 miles of open water between Lae and Howland Island. Earhart's Lockheed Electra rolled down the runway at 10 a.m. on July 2.

Over the next twenty hours, Earhart was in sporadic radio contact with her support ship near Howland. For most of that period, things seemed to be on track. But sometime during the night, Earhart and Noonan drifted off course. The last faint transmission came at 8:43 a.m. Then there was silence. For sixteen days, ships and planes canvassed a Texas-sized piece of the Pacific without finding a single sign of the plane or crew.

Tragically, she is now remembered more for her disappearance than her record-shattering career in aviation or her tremendous spirit. "She was," said one eulogist "in rebellion against a world which had been made, for women, too safe, too unexciting. She wanted to dare all that a man would dare."

❦

GRACE HOPPER

DECEMBER 9, 1906–JANUARY 1, 1992

AMERICAN

Known as "Amazing Grace" and "the first lady of software", pioneering computer programmer Grace Hopper is best remembered for helping to create the first all-electronic digital computer, UNIVAC (Universal Automatic Computer).

Hopper was born in New York and later attended Vassar College. She graduated in 1928 with a mathematics degree, then received master's and doctorate degrees in mathematics and physics from Yale University in 1934.

During World War II, at the age of 37, she enlisted with the Women Accepted for Volunteer Emergency Service (WAVES). She trained at the Naval Reserve Midshipmen's School at Smith College in Northampton, Massachusetts, and graduated top of her class in 1944. From there, she was assigned to the Bureau of Ships Computation Project at Harvard University as a lieutenant, junior grade.

It was as an employee of Eckert-Mauchly Computer Corporation that Hopper undertook pioneering work in compiling mathematic code into a language. Her assistance in developing the first computer compiler and the first computer programming language (COBOL) helped to revolutionize the world of computers.

Due to her invaluable knowledge, at the age of 60, she was recalled to active duty with the Navy to tackle standardizing communication between different computer languages. She would remain there for 19 years, retiring as an admiral at the age of 79.

In addition to her programming accomplishments, Hopper's legacy includes encouraging young women to learn how to program. The annual "Grace Hopper Celebration" is the world's largest technical conference for women in computing, and her legacy continues to serve as a role model and inspiration to women working in a variety of science, technology, engineering, and mathematics (STEM) fields today.

STEPHANIE KWOLEK

JULY 31, 1923–JUNE 18, 2014

AMERICAN-POLISH

Stephanie Kwolek is the chemist who created Kevlar. Not only is Kevlar a multi-purpose synthetic material used to fortify a variety of products, this champion of the chemical world also continues to save lives through its use in protective clothing and headgear.

Some say the best form of attack is defense. With that in mind, Kevlar is crucial to the protection of our modern-day heroes, from riot squads to front-line soldiers. Like the plate-metal armor of medieval knights, Kevlar can really take a hit. Luckily, unlike Sir Lancelot's heavy armor, our warriors' protection is a lot less clunky and cumbersome.

Since its creation in 1965, by American chemist Stephanie Kwolek, Kevlar has been put to all manner of different uses. It is a high-strength, low-weight material made from a chemical known as a polyamide, which is five times stronger than steel. It is also non-flammable, chemically resistant, and highly durable.

As a fiber, it functions as a lightweight reinforcement in ropes, cables, and protective gloves, and is used to strengthen tires and hoses. Kevlar threads can also be used to increase the effectiveness of fire-resistant items such as mattresses, and are an integral part of fire-fighter uniforms, owing to their ability to withstand scorching temperatures.

More poignantly, it is used in the armored vehicles, bulletproof vests, and helmets that protect our world's policeman, security, armies – you name it. This is possible because of the revolutionary high-strength and lightweight properties of Kevlar.

SPACE AND THE ENVIRONMENT

❧

Henrietta Leavitt

❧

Rachel Carson

❧

Dian Fossey

❧

Jane Goodall

❧

Valentina Tereshkova

❧

Jocelyn Bell Burnell

HENRIETTA LEAVITT

JULY 4, 1868–DECEMBER 12, 1921

AMERICAN

Astronomer Henrietta Leavitt is probably best known for discovering the relation between the luminosity and the period of Cepheid variable stars – a way of deciding whether stars are dim or just far away. A triumph for female scientists whose work, deemed by Edwin Hubble, was worthy of a receiving a Nobel Prize.

By the late nineteenth century, computers had become available to astronomers. At that time, however, these "computers" were not machines, but women – employed to carry out the drudge tasks that the main researchers didn't want to do themselves. Henrietta Leavitt was one of these women – a group assembled by Harvard astronomer Edward Pickering, coined "Pickering's Harem".

Henrietta Leavitt worked in the Harvard astronomy department from 1895 until her death in 1921, during which time she discovered a vast array of variable stars – stars that changed their brightness at a fixed rate. Through years of close study, Leavitt found that the brighter stars pulsed more slowly and, what's more, a star's pulse rate could be used to calculate how bright it actually was. For the first time, astronomers could work out whether a star was dim because it was a long way away or because it was... well, just not very bright.

This was the yardstick that allowed other astronomers, notably Edwin Hubble, to make their important contributions to our knowledge of the Universe. The relationship later proved so important that she was considered for a Nobel Prize. Unfortunately, her untimely death in 1921 rendered her and her work unable to receive the prize, due to the "rule" that they're not awarded posthumously.

However, because of her findings, measurements derived from variable stars have provided evidence for the changing shape and size of the Universe. Henrietta Leavitt broke boundaries, saw through illness, and the experience of being deaf, to provide key discoveries in astronomy.

RACHEL CARSON

MAY 27, 1907–APRIL 14, 1964

AMERICAN

Rachel Carson is the marine biologist, author, and conservationist considered to be one of the pioneers of modern environmentalism.

Born in 1907, on a farm in the rural Pennsylvanian town of Springdale, Rachel Carson fed her love of nature early in life by exploring the forests and streams of her hometown. After a brief stint as an English student at Pennsylvania College for Women, she switched her focus to biology, and eventually earned her master's degree in zoology at Johns Hopkins University.

After being hired by the United States Fish and Wildlife Service in 1935, to write seven-minute radio spots about marine life, entitled "Romance Under the Waters," Carson went on to publish numerous freelance articles on the wonder of nature and man's place among it. Her poetic, yet scientifically enlightening style, was revealed in her first book *Under the Sea Wind* (1941), and more famously in *The Sea Around Us* (1952). The latter placed her on the *New York Times* Bestseller List and won her the coveted National Book Award.

In 1962, Carson published probably her best-known work, the controversial book *Silent Spring*, which exposed the public to the dangers of pesticides used by the government and agricultural industries. The chemical industry and other opponents blasted her personally and professionally; however, the new concern over pesticides led to a Congressional hearing in 1963, and a subsequent ban on widespread use of a particularly dangerous chemical, dichlorodiphenyltrichloroethane, known as DDT.

Carson died in 1964, after a battle with breast cancer, but left in her wake an enduring awareness of environmentalism, the likes of which had never before been observed in America.

DIAN FOSSEY

JANUARY 16, 1932–DECEMBER 26, 1985

AMERICAN

Primatologist Dian Fossey was made a household name and introduced people to the plight of the endangered mountain gorilla, after a picture of her made the cover of *National Geographic*.

In three years of studying the mountain gorilla in the Rwandan jungles, primatologist Dian Fossey had learned that the best way to get close to her skittish subjects was to try to fit in. So when a young blackback named Peanuts approached her one morning, she acted like a gorilla, loudly scratching her scalp and leaning casually back into the dense foliage.

She slowly extended a hand. And then, after contemplating it for a moment, Peanuts did something none of his species had ever done before: he reached out and touched her fingers with his own. They sat for a moment, holding hands, until "he stood and gave vent to his excitement by a whirling chest beat, then went off to rejoin his group," she wrote in her journal. "I expressed my own happy excitement by crying..."

Peanuts and Fossey were not alone that morning. *National Geographic* photographer Bob Campbell, who had been documenting Fossey's research activities in Rwanda since 1968, was just out of view. His photos became the magazine's cover story in early 1970 and brought enormous public interest to Fossey's cause.

Fossey used her newfound fame to draw attention to the need for conservation and protection of her endangered subjects. But her compassion for the gorilla led to contempt for humans, particularly poachers and government officials who wanted to exploit the animals for financial gain. Fossey was found brutally murdered in her cabin at her Karisoke Research Center two days after Christmas in 1985, and yet her legacy is one that has changed conservation efforts forever.

JANE GOODALL

APRIL 3, 1934

BRITISH

Primatologist Jane Goodall singlehandedly
revolutionized the branch of zoology that studies
the behavior of animals in their natural habitats.
The discoveries she has made and the way she
has changed public and scientific perceptions of
chimps are huge.

Jane Goodall, born in Hampstead, England, in 1934, to a businessman father and novelist mother, has achieved much more than for what she is best know – her work as a primatologist. As well as being only the eighth person in Cambridge University's history to have been awarded a doctorate without a bachelor's degree, she set up the Jane Goodall Institute, now a powerful conservation body.

In 1960, Goodall started studying chimps in the Kakombe Valley, Tanzania, a feat in itself at a time when it was almost unheard of for women to head off into the wilds of the African forest. Her first task was simply to acclimatize the chimps to her presence, so that she could start to study their behavior. She defied scientific convention by giving the chimps names instead of numbers, and revolutionized both the way they were studied, and the accepted knowledge about their behavior.

Goodall unmasked complex, emotional behaviors such as adoption, tool-making, and even warfare, and insisted on the validity of her observations that animals have distinct personalities, minds, and emotions.

The Jane Goodall Institute was set up in 1977 to provide continuing support for chimpanzee research in Africa. Today, its mission is to advance the power of individuals to take informed and compassionate action to improve the environment for all living things. Now with nineteen centers around the world, the institute is a leader in the effort to protect chimpanzees and their habitats, and is widely recognized for establishing innovative community-centered conservation and development programs across Africa.

❦

VALENTINA TERESHKOVA

MARCH 6, 1937

RUSSIAN

Winner of the "Greatest Women Achiever of the Century" award in 2000, cosmonaut Valentina Tereshkova, as the first woman in space, reached new heights in terms of both exploration and equality.

On June 16, 1963, and after being selected from over 400 applicants, the Soviet Union's Valentina Tereshkova became the first woman to fly into space aboard the Vostok 6 mission, just two years after Yuri Gagarin had made man's maiden space flight. Being an expert parachutist – she had made over 125 jumps before entering space-flight training school – helped in her selection and training as a cosmonaut in 1962.

She was originally selected as the pilot for *Vostok 6*'s twin, *Vostok 5*, with fellow female hopeful Valentina Ponomareva set to follow in *Vostok 6*, but a change of plan saw a male cosmonaut take over duties in the first of the two linked missions. Two days after *Vostok 5* went into orbit, *Vostok 6*, piloted by Tereshkova, blasted off into space with the other female candidates looking on. During the mission, Tereshkova traveled round the Earth forty-eight times, and spent a total of nearly three days in space.

On her successful return to Earth, she became a cosmonaut engineer, and later went into politics, becoming a prominent member of the Soviet government. She is much decorated, receiving the prestigious Hero of the Soviet Union – Russia's highest honorary title – in 1963.

She was also voted the "Greatest Woman Achiever of the Century," awarded in London, in 2000, at the Annual Women's Assembly. There is a moon crater named after her and Tereshkova now heads the Russian government's Center for International Scientific and Cultural Co-operation.

JOCELYN BELL BURNELL

JULY 15, 1943

BRITISH

Astrophysicist Jocelyn Bell Burnell's discovery added further insight into the phenomenon of collapsed stars, and spawned a whole field of study around neutron pulsars.

Jocelyn Bell Burnell was studying at Cambridge University in 1967, under the guidance of Antony Hewish, when she discovered a regular, pulsing radio emission emanating from outer space; jokingly, she labeled it "Little Green Men 1" on charts. It was later discovered to be a radio pulsar – a fast-spinning collapsed star – and Hewish's team published their findings in a scientific paper. Discovery turned to controversy, however, as Hewish and co-author Martin Ryle later won the Nobel Prize in Physics to the exclusion of Bell Burnell, a decision debated ever since.

Bell Burnell joined Hewish's team after completing a physics degree at Glasgow University in 1965, helping to build a massive radio telescope to study the phenomenon of quasars while studying for her Ph.D. at Cambridge in 1967. She soon noticed a series of repeating radio emissions on the printouts, occurring just over once every second – too frequent to be from a quasar. The team realized the emissions must be coming from rapidly spinning celestial corpses called neutron stars – the collapsed remnants of a dead star.

The discovery prompted a flurry of media attention and the discovery of more pulsars, and Bell Burnell earned her Ph.D. in 1968. In 1974, the Nobel committee rewarded Hewish and Ryle, leaving out Bell Burnell, a move that angered cosmologist Fred Hoyle. Bell Burnell remained unconcerned, however, and went on to study astronomy at various U.K. institutions.

Her work is remembered as an important discovery in the modern description of our Universe, later acting as further evidence for the existence of black holes.

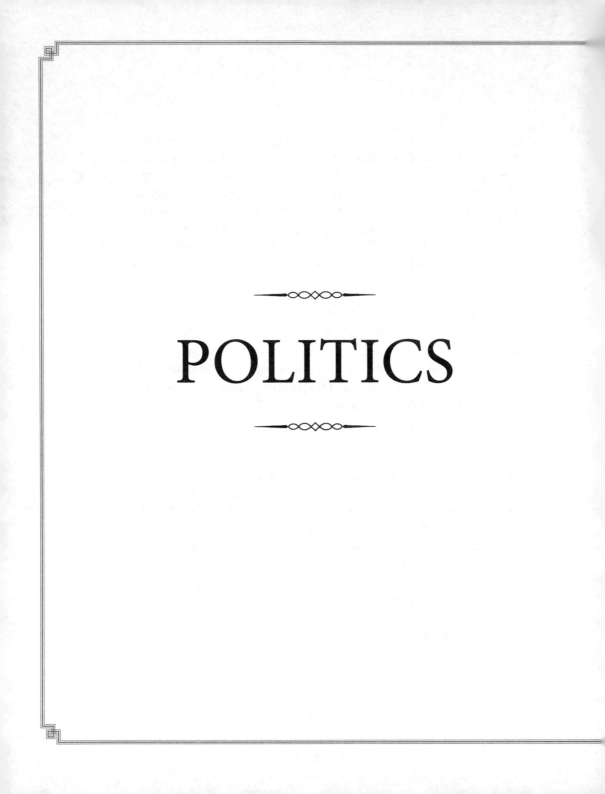

POLITICS

Jeannette Rankin

Eleanor Roosevelt

Indira Gandhi

Margaret Thatcher

Angela Davis

Hillary Clinton

Benazir Bhutto

Angela Merkel

Condoleezza Rice

Julia Eileen Gillard

Michelle Obama

JEANNETTE RANKIN

JUNE 11, 1880–MAY 18, 1973

AMERICAN

Women's-rights activist, pacifist, and politician Jeannette Rankin was the first woman to be elected to the U.S. Congress. During her time in the House of Representatives, she helped pass the 19th Amendment, giving women the right to vote.

Jeannette Rankin, the eldest daughter of a rancher and a schoolteacher, was born near Missoula, Montana, in 1880. She graduated from the University of Montana in 1902, then attended the New York School of Philanthropy, before embarking on a career in social work in Spokane, Washington. Finding social work unsatisfying, she instead entered the University of Washington. It was here that she joined the women's suffrage movement and, in 1914, became legislative secretary of the National American Woman Suffrage Association.

In 1916, she was elected to the U.S. House of Representatives, becoming the first woman to hold a seat in either chamber. In office, she supported the federal women's suffrage amendment, measures to protect women workers, mothers, and children. But it was possibly her pacifism that caused the greatest stir – she was an outspoken isolationist and, in 1917, voted against declaring war on Germany: "I want to stand by my country, but I cannot vote for war," she declared. This effectively ruined her chances of re-election the following year.

She was, however, elected once again, in 1940, but voted against the declaration of war on Japan after the Pearl Harbor invasion. This unpopular stance terminated her political career.

Rankin continued to campaign into her 90s and served as a huge inspiration to the next generations of pacifists, female politicians, feminists, and civil-rights advocates.

ELEANOR ROOSEVELT

OCTOBER 11, 1884–NOVEMBER 7, 1962

AMERICAN

The longest-serving First Lady of the United States, Eleanor Roosevelt drafted the Declaration of Human Rights, which was the first global statement on human rights.

On the day the Universal Declaration of Human Rights (UDHR) was signed at the Palais de Chaillot in Paris, Eleanor Roosevelt proclaimed that it "may well become the international Magna Carta of all men everywhere." The former First Lady had chaired the committee that drafted the document. She was the only member of the committee that was not a scholar or expert in international relations, but had approached her job as chairperson with her customary determination.

"We wanted as many nations as possible to accept the fact that men, for one reason or another, were born free and equal in dignity and rights, that they were endowed with reason and conscience, and should act toward one another in a spirit of brotherhood," she once said. "The way to do that was to find words that everyone would accept."

But as deliberations over the UDHR began in Paris that winter, it was clear that acceptance was far from universal. Members of the Islamic states argued that the declaration was dominated by Western values. Some Westerners thought it was too socialist, while Soviet delegates thought it wasn't socialist enough, and the Vatican complained that God was not mentioned. When it finally passed, it was not unanimous. The final vote was 48–0 and 8 abstentions, with the Soviet Bloc, the Saudis, and South Africa refusing to sign on.

Today, the UDHR holds the Guinness World Record title for the "most translated" document, having been published in well over 300 languages.

INDIRA GANDHI

NOVEMBER 19, 1917–OCTOBER 31, 1984

INDIAN

The first and only female prime minister of India to date, Indira Gandhi's political career saw India rise to regional-power status while flirting with authoritarian excess, highlighting the country's social and political fault lines for two tense decades.

Indira Gandhi united in her slight, apparently unassuming person a number of remarkable achievements and contradictions. Born to Jawaharlal Nehru, the first prime minister of India, Gandhi was the recipient at birth of an immense political capital that she spent expertly over the years, beginning with her election to the presidency of the Indian National Congress in 1959 and continuing on to her election as prime minister on January 19, 1966.

Soon after her election, Gandhi parted ways from the legacy of her father and his gently democratic generation of Indian freedom fighters, and began to evince authoritarian tendencies that peaked during her 1975 seizure of emergency powers and her persecution of Sikhs in the early 1980s.

Uncomfortable with dissent in general and regional power brokers in particular, Gandhi was thus particularly upset by Sikh separatists in the Punjab and famously attacked them in the Golden Temple in Amritsar in 1984. Soon afterwards, her own Sikh bodyguards gunned her down in retaliation.

Despite her unpalatable moments of authoritarianism, Gandhi nonetheless employed her two decades of power to guide India toward nuclear power (India first detonated an atomic bomb in 1974), greater agricultural production, and overall economic gains. India first became a world player under Gandhi's scrupulous watch and, through the political careers of her children, daughter-in-law, Sonia Gandhi, and other relatives, she has continued to cast a long shadow over India even after her death.

❦

MARGARET THATCHER

OCTOBER 13, 1925–APRIL 8, 2013

BRITISH

Margaret Thatcher was a British Member of Parliament who, having become leader of the Conservative Party in 1975, served as the U.K.'s Prime Minister from 1979 to 1990. As well as being the first woman to lead a political party in the U.K., she was the country's first female Prime Minister, and its longest serving of the 20th-century.

Margaret Thatcher was born into a humble Lincolnshire family in 1925. School reports reveal her as having been a hard worker not only in the classroom, but within extra-curricular activities such as swimming, playing the piano, and field hockey. Her hard work paid off when she won a scholarship to Kesteven and Grantham Girls' School, which paved the way to her attendance of Oxford University. An unusual start to a political career, Thatcher studied chemistry under the supervision of Dorothy Hodgkin, leading her to becoming the first U.K. prime minister with a science degree.

At Oxford, she became President of the Oxford Conservative Association and, after her studies, joined the local Conservative Association, securing herself as the Conservative candidate for Dartford, attracting much media attention in the process as the youngest and only female candidate. Despite losses, and wins, and her subsequent qualification as a barrister, Thatcher eventually succeeded in becoming a Member of Parliament. Her stint as Education Secretary under Edward Heath from 1970 to 1974 which paved the way to her succeeding him as leader of the Conservative party in 1975, and becoming prime minister in 1979.

As Prime Minister, Thatcher battled the country's recession and caused mixed feelings from across the UK with her reputation as the "Iron Lady", of which she embraced. She made controversial decisions to privatize social housing and public transport, and even in her government she took on the trade unions, requiring them to hold a secret ballot before any work stoppage, refusing to make any concessions during a yearlong miners' strike.

Even after her resignation in November 1990 and despite her strong will, leadership traits, and often negative connotations, Margaret Thatcher remains one of the most influential and powerful women of the 20th century, proving that women can be politicians, and tough enough to take on all criticisms.

ANGELA DAVIS

JANUARY 26, 1944

AMERICAN

Political activist, writer, and scholar, Angela Davis has made it her life's work to combat all forms of oppression in the U.S. and around the world. Active from a young age in the Black Panthers and the American Communist Party, she now lectures in many prestigious universities, discussing issues regarding race, the criminal justice system, and gender equality.

Davis was brought up in middle-class Alabama, in a segregated neighborhood that taught her much about racial prejudice. As a teenager, she rebelled and organized interracial study groups, that the police disbanded. In the late 1960s, as a graduate student at the University of California, she became actively involved in the Black Panthers and the Che-Lumumba Club, the all-black branch of the American Communist Party. She was later hired to teach philosophy at the university, but was fired because of her association with communism.

In the early 1970s, Davis became involved in the campaign to free the Soledad Brothers – three men who were accused of killing a prison guard after several African-American inmates had been killed in a fight by another guard – which led to her own arrest and imprisonment. During her high-profile trial in 1972, Davis was acquitted on all charges. She remains an advocate of prison abolition to this day and is a powerful voice against racism within the criminal justice system.

Despite former California Governor Ronald Reagan once vowing that Angela Davis would never again teach in the University of California system, she became a lecturer in women's and ethnic studies at San Francisco State University in 1977, and is now Distinguished Professor Emerita in the History of Consciousness and Feminist Studies Departments at the University of California.

Davis has written several books and continues to lecture on race, women's rights, and the criminal justice system. In 2017, she was a featured speaker and made honorary co-chair at the Women's March on Washington after Donald Trump's inauguration. Hers is a voice that refused to be silenced and continues to be heard today, loud and clear.

HILLARY CLINTON

OCTOBER 26, 1947

AMERICAN

As former First Lady of the United States, Hillary Rodham Clinton has since come to be well respected for a political and legal career in her own right, and as the first female candidate of a major political party to run for the U.S. presidency.

Hillary Rodham Clinton was born in Chicago, Illinois, in 1947, and was brought up in a politically conservative household, with parents who wanted her to have an independent and professional career. Clinton followed this path by way of attending Wellesley College in Massachusetts, majoring in political science, before entering Yale Law School, where her involvement stretched far beyond her participation in the classroom – from serving on the editorial board of the *Yale Review of Law and Social Action* to volunteering at New Haven Legal Services, for which she offered free legal advice to the poor and vulnerable.

It was at Yale, in 1971, where she met Bill Clinton and, after repeated requests for her to marry him, she said yes and they moved to Arkansas, where she became one of only two female faculty members in the School of Law at its university. As well as teaching criminal law, she also became the director of a new legal-aid clinic at the school, whilst her husband pursued his own political career, leading, in 1993, to his becoming the 42nd President of the United States.

With her pull into the spotlight, Clinton continued to play an active role in various areas of social reform. Her work as First Lady touched upon areas of national healthcare reform, human rights, and women's rights in America and across the globe, and she continued to do so after leaving the White House – first as New York Senator, then as U.S. Secretary of State under Barack Obama, and, more recently, as the Democratic Party's nominee for President in 2016 – the first woman to have received such a nomination.

Clinton's presidential campaign focused on issues such as expanding racial, LGBT, and women's rights, raising wages and ensuring equal pay for women, and improving healthcare. However, despite holding a significant lead through the national polls throughout most of 2016, Clinton was defeated to the presidency by Donald Trump. Yet, Hillary Clinton remains as a voice that has inspired and been of tremendous influence in female history.

BENAZIR BHUTTO

JUNE 21, 1953–DECEMBER 27, 2007

PAKISTANI

Benazir Bhutto was the first democratically elected female leader of a Muslim country. She fought tirelessly for democracy and human rights, ruling with an uncompromising approach that earned her the nickname the "Iron Lady of Pakistan."

Benazir Bhutto was born in Karachi, Pakistan, in 1953. She was the eldest child of Zulfikar Ali Bhutto, founder of the Pakistan People's Party (PPP) and the country's prime minister, 1973–1977. She moved to the U.S. in 1969 to complete her education at Harvard University, graduating in 1973 with a degree in comparative government. Next, she moved to the U.K. where she studied philosophy, political science, and economics at the University of Oxford.

Bhutto returned to Pakistan in 1977 and, following her father's execution in 1979 at the hands of the military dictator Mohammad Zia-ul-Haq, became head of the PPP. She endured frequent house arrests under the rule of President Zia and was exiled from 1984 to 1986. After the lifting of martial law, Bhutto returned to Pakistan and soon became the foremost figure in political opposition to Zia, campaigning for free elections and a representative government. She rallied her people and attracted large crowds of followers, becoming prime minister in 1988. She took great strides forward in restoring basic human rights to her people and also brought about several political and economic policies for industrial development and growth.

However, she struggled to clean up governmental corruption. In 1990, President Khan ousted Bhutto from her position as prime minister using the Eighth Amendment, citing charges of corruption, nepotism, and despotism. In 1993, she was re-elected but was again removed in 1996, this time by President Farooq Leghari. After conceding defeat in the 1997 elections, she went into self-imposed exile in Dubai in 1998.

In 2007, Bhutto struck a deal with President Musharraf and returned to Pakistan. Thousands showed up to welcome her and she looked set for another victory at the polls, but the political violence she had tried to subdue throughout her career claimed her life when she was assassinated that same year. She was later named one of seven winners of the United Nations Prize in the Field of Human Rights and stands as a figure of great strength, having exerted her right to rule in a male-dominated society.

ANGELA MERKEL

JULY 17, 1954

GERMAN

Angela Merkel, the first female chancellor of Germany, is widely described as the de facto leader of the European Union and the most powerful woman in the world. Her leadership style is one of stability, pragmatism, and fundamental decency.

Angela Merkel grew up with her Lutheran pastor father and her mother, who was a teacher, in the countryside north of East Berlin. She later studied physics at the University of Leipzig, earning a doctorate in quantum chemistry, then worked as a chemist at the Central Institute for Physical Chemistry, Academy of Sciences from 1978 to 1990.

Merkel entered politics in 1989 after the fall of the Berlin Wall. Following German reunification in 1990, she was elected to the Bundestag and rose rapidly in the CDU (Christian Democratic Union) party, becoming leader of the opposition in 2002.

Following the 2005 national elections, Merkel became Germany's first female chancellor and went on to become one of the architects of reform to the European Union. She was re-elected in 2009, 2013, and 2017, the latter heralding her fourth consecutive term as chancellor.

Despite a smaller margin in the 2017 election, Merkel topped that year's *Forbes'* list of the most powerful women in the world for the seventh year running. Between the two poles of Vladimir Putin's authoritarian populism and Donald Trump's nationalism, many regard Angela Merkel as the last real democratic leader standing.

❦

CONDOLEEZZA RICE

NOVEMBER 14, 1954

AMERICAN

Politician and educator, Condoleezza Rice was the first African-American woman to serve as U.S. Secretary of State (from 2005–2009). She was often cited as the most powerful woman in global politics.

The only child of a Presbyterian minister and a teacher, Condoleezza Rice was born in 1954 in Birmingham, Alabama, into a segregated society. In spite of early ambitions to become a concert pianist, she instead studied political science, receiving her master's degree from the University of Notre Dame. She completed her Ph.D. in political science at the University of Denver in 1981.

As professor of political science at Stanford University, Rice won two of the highest teaching honors – the 1984 Walter J. Gores Award for Excellence in Teaching and the 1993 School of Humanities and Sciences Dean's Award for Distinguished Teaching. Rice later became the first female, first black and youngest Provost of Stanford.

In 1999, Rice left Stanford to become foreign-policy advisor to the presidential campaign of George W. Bush, and upon his election , was named head of the NSC (National Security Council), the first woman to hold this position. She went on to prove to be an important and influential advisor to Bush.

She championed the idea of "Transformational Diplomacy," which sought to redistribute U.S. diplomats to areas of severe social and political trouble, and helped successfully negotiate several agreements in the Middle East.

JULIA EILEEN GILLARD

SEPTEMBER 29, 1961

AUSTRALIAN

Julia Eileen Gillard became Australia's first female prime minister, deftly and graciously wading through the minefield of gender politics to lead her country.

Gillard was born in 1961 in Barry, Wales, but she suffered from bronchopneumonia as a child and her parents were advised to move her to a warmer climate to aid her recovery. So they made the decision to migrate to Adelaide in Australia in 1966, and it was there, at university, that Gillard was introduced to politics, by the daughter of a State Labor Minister, and joined the Labor Club. She then moved to Melbourne University, where she led the Australian Union of Students (only the second woman to have done so) and studied law.

At the age of 29, Gillard became a partner in law the firm Slater & Gordon, where she specialized in industrial law, leaving in 1996 to work as chief of staff to Victorian ALP leader John Brumby. She was first elected to the House of Representatives at the 1998 federal election representing Labor. In 2001, she was elevated to the front bench and given the shadow portfolio of population and immigration, adeptly reshaping the ALP's unpopular policy on immigration.

An overwhelming ALP victory in the 2007 federal elections led to Gillard's promotion to Australia's first-ever female deputy prime minister, to Prime Minister Kevin Rudd. Declining poll numbers and a lack of confidence in Rudd's leadership from within the party led Gillard to challenge for the leadership.

On June 24 2010, Gillard was sworn in as Australia's first female prime minister. Her political career has not been an easy one but she leaves a legacy of social, education and health reforms, and has proved that it is possible for a woman to claim the top spot in Australian politics.

MICHELLE OBAMA

JANUARY 17, 1964

AMERICAN

Michelle Obama served as America's first African-American First Lady from 2009 to 2017, and championed for a healthier and more educated nation. As a Harvard-educated lawyer, a feminist, a mother and a dynamic public speaker, she has become an inspiration to women across the globe.

Michelle Obama was born in Chicago, Illinois, in1964. She was a gifted student who attended Princeton University, before going on to study law at Harvard. After graduation, she worked in a Chicago law firm, where she met future President of the United States, Barack Obama, who she married in 1992.

In 1993, Obama left law to pursue a career in public service, initially working as an assistant to Chicago's mayor. She later became executive director for the Chicago Office of Public Allies, a nonprofit leadership-training program that helped young adults develop skills for future careers in the public sector. In 1996, Obama joined the University of Chicago as associate dean of student services and, in 2005, she was appointed vice president for community and external affairs at the University of Chicago Medical Center.

As First Lady, a role she undertook with honesty, humour, dignity, and kindness, Obama became an inspiring presence. She visited homeless shelters and soup kitchens, she championed a number of worthy causes, including poverty awareness, support for military families, education, women's rights, and nutrition to combat the epidemic of childhood obesity.

As a young mother, a fashion icon, a skilled speaker, and the first African-American First Lady, Michelle Obama has become a well-deserved role model.

CULTURE AND SOCIETY

Queen Victoria

Helena Rubinstein

Helen Keller

Coco Chanel

Margaret Mead

Marlene Dietrich

Simone de Beauvoir

Betty Friedan

Queen Elizabeth II

Audrey Hepburn

Jacqueline Kennedy Onassis

Mary Quant

Germaine Greer

Alice Walker

Caitlyn Jenner

Oprah Winfrey

Diana, Princess of Wales

Sheryl Sandberg

Audrey Pulvar

Chimamanda Ngozi Adichie

QUEEN VICTORIA

MAY 24, 1819–JANUARY 22 ,1901

BRITISH

Queen Victoria is the second-longest reigning British monarch, after Queen Elizabeth II. She was the first and last Empress of India and the last British monarch of the House of Hanover, her death marking the end of the Victorian era.

Victoria was born at Kensington Palace, London, on May 24, 1819, and, on the death of William IV, in 1837, became Queen at the relatively young age of eighteen. She reigned over what was seen as a triumphant age of industrial expansion and economic progress. The British Empire became the dominant global power, to such an extent that, by the time of her death, it was said that Britain had an empire on which the sun never set.

In 1840, she married Prince Albert, who is best remembered for his conception of the Great Exhibition of 1851. Victoria was a busy mother as well as the reigning monarch, bearing nine children between 1840 and 1857. Their children's marriages into other royal families helped to spread the influence of Victorian Britain. Victoria's popularity grew in tandem with increasing imperial sentiment and what would now be described as racism and xenophobia.

Nevertheless, it was during her reign that political power gradually diffused to the electorate, and the modern concept of a constitutional monarchy as a more nominal figure above political parties was born. However, Victoria herself would not waive the opportunity to voice her opinions, if sometimes in private, and never distanced herself from political life.

She continued her duties right until her death at Osborne House on the Isle of Wight, on January 22, 1901. Her reign lasted almost sixty-four years, the second-longest in British history.

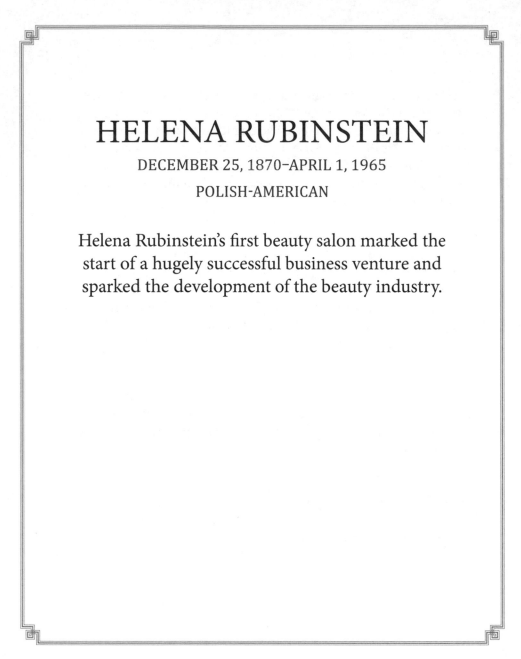

HELENA RUBINSTEIN

DECEMBER 25, 1870–APRIL 1, 1965

POLISH-AMERICAN

Helena Rubinstein's first beauty salon marked the start of a hugely successful business venture and sparked the development of the beauty industry.

As with her beauty products, there are many elements of Helena Rubinstein's life story that remain unproven; much of the mythology about her was self-promulgated. What is true, though, is that Rubinstein's establishment of a beauty salon in Melbourne, Australia, in 1902, marked the beginnings of the multibillion-dollar beauty industry.

Rubinstein was born in Kraków, Poland, in 1870, and was the eldest of eight children. She moved to Australia in 1894, possibly to avoid a marriage that her father had arranged. There, she began to produce a quasi-medical concoction that she called "Crème Valaze." Rubinstein maintained that it was made from a rare mountain herb, and her own peachy complexion aided its popularity. She soon set up a beauty salon, which had an "operating theater," and claimed to cure everything from warts to double chins, as well as poor skin. The business was successful from the start.

In 1905, Rubinstein went to Europe to study skin treatment with European specialists. Her business continued to prosper. She lived first in London and then in Paris, marketing her products in each city. When World War I broke out, she left Paris and traveled to New York. Her rivalry with Florence Nightingale Graham (Elizabeth Arden) and Charles Revson, who founded Revlon, was well known.

Rubinstein died in April, 1965. At that time, her business was worth more than U.S.$60 million.

HELEN KELLER

JUNE 27, 1880–JUNE 1, 1968

AMERICAN

By publishing her autobiography, *The Story of My Life*, deaf-blind Helen Keller became an international celebrity. This, her first book, documents her extraordinary achievement in learning to communicate and acquire a thorough education as the first deaf-blind person to earn a bachelor of arts degree.

If Helen Keller had not lost her sight and hearing after suffering a high fever, at the tragically young age of nineteen months, then she would probably have remained unknown to most of the world's population. The following five frustrating years were spent in a dark, isolated world, and as she was unable to see or hear, Keller also became mute. In desperation, her parents consulted the Scottish inventor and expert on deafness, Alexander Graham Bell, who recommended Anne Sullivan (Macy) as a suitable teacher for Keller.

As she had also been partially blind during her short life, Sullivan had a loyal empathy with Keller and would spell the words of objects on to Helen's palms. Ravenous for more knowledge, Keller learned to "hear" conversations by placing her hands on the face and throat of the speaker. She was soon reading Braille and using a specially adapted typewriter to write.

Having developed communication skills never previously achieved by any similarly disabled person, Keller began to write on many subjects for journals, and later published several books about her life. Keller's publications and the subsequent fundraising by both Sullivan and herself were beneficial in preventing the practice of automatically placing all blind and deaf children in institutions for life.

As an influential example of what an educated disabled person could achieve, Keller was able to convince powerful members of society of the value of appropriate education for disabled children and thus dramatically improve their futures and quality of life. In her own words, "Once I knew only darkness and stillness … but a little word from the fingers of another … and my heart leaped to the rapture of living."

COCO CHANEL

AUGUST 19, 1883–JANUARY 10, 1971

FRENCH

Coco Chanel was a revered style icon and fashion designer who ruled over Parisian haute couture. Her timeless designs, trademark suits, and little black dresses changed the face of fashion and still shape what we wear today.

Coco Chanel was born Gabrielle Bonheur Chanel in Saumur, France. Whilst she was to become synonymous with glamour, her early years of poverty were anything but. After her mother's death, her father, who worked as a peddler, put her in an orphanage. She was raised by nuns and it is here where she learnt to sew, a skill that would change the course of her life.

Chanel worked for a few years singing cabaret, where she gained her nickname "Coco," but her fashion career began in 1910 on Paris's Rue Cambon, the location of her first shop, selling hats, financed by her latest in a string of wealthy lovers, Boy Capel. She soon expanded her business with stores in Deauville and Biarritz and began making clothes. Chanel's designs, in contrast to the stifling corseted styles prevalent at the time, stressed simplicity and comfort and revolutionized the fashion industry.

Through the 1920s Chanel took her already thriving business to new heights with the launch of her signature scent Chanel No. 5, the first time a perfume had ever featured the name of its creator. Then, in 1925, inspired by menswear, she introduced her now legendary suit for women, comprising of a collarless jacket and a fitted skirt. Next came the sophisticated and chic little black dress – staple party wear to this very day.

The economic depression of the 1930s slowed down her commercial endeavours, but it was the outbreak of World War II that forced Chanel to shut her business. During the German occupation of France, she courted controversy through her involvement with German military officer, Hans Gunther von Dincklage. Although not officially charged as a collaborator, many believed her to have betrayed her country. As a result, Chanel spent several years in Switzerland. Yet, at the age of 70, Coco Chanel made a triumphant return to the fashion world, where she once again wowed with her styles of sophisticated simplicity.

MARGARET MEAD

DECEMBER 16, 1901–NOVEMBER 15, 1978

AMERICAN

From her work as cultural anthropologist, Margaret Mead produced the famous and groundbreaking book, *Coming of Age in Samoa*, which – rightly or wrongly – challenged the existing perceptions of adolescent sexuality.

The American cultural anthropologist Margaret Mead was only twenty-four when she spent nine months in Samoa, observing the sexual experiences of young girls on Ta'u Island. Mead's colorful and highly readable account of her findings became one of the most widely known anthropological texts ever written. It was also one of the most influential.

Mead painted a compelling picture of a close-knit and well-adjusted society, where sex was a natural and positive experience, and starkly contrasted this with the repressive social mores that prevailed in the United States at that time. The book had a huge impact on contemporary theories of childrearing, and contributed, at least indirectly, to the emergence of far more permissive attitudes to sex in Western society.

Yet, *Coming of Age in Samoa* is now one of the most controversial texts of its time and kind. While Samoans have found her descriptions of their culture misleading and insulting, scientists have questioned the scientific accuracy of Mead's methods. She has been accused of altering or even fabricating the evidence to fit her own preconceived theories. One of her greatest critics was Derek Freeman, an anthropology professor from New Zealand.

In various works published after her death, Freeman claimed that some of the girls Mead worked with had admitted to him that the stories they'd told her were either lies or jokes, undermining Mead's hypotheses about Samoan sexuality. However, several of Freeman's conclusions have also been disputed, and the whole debate remains both lively and influential, if unresolved.

MARLENE DIETRICH

DECEMBER 27, 1901–MAY 6, 1992

GERMAN

By refusing to accept traditional female film roles, and constantly reinventing herself – on and off screen – Marlene Dietrich became a role model for women, leading the way for other female actors to challenge and break convention.

A sound-film star with silent-movie film-star looks, Marlene Dietrich's role as "Lola Lola" in the 1930 Josef von Sternberg film *The Blue Angel* made her famous overnight. Playing a nightclub singer whose performance is so spectacular that an aging professor leaves his career to follow her, Dietrich helped define the role of femme fatale that became a staple of Hollywood films in the 1930s and 1940s.

But as Dietrich showed in *Morocco* – her follow-up to *The Blue Angel* – she was more than just a character type. Working again with von Sternberg, who collaborated with her on seven films in five years, Dietrich established herself as an actress willing to flout convention. In *Morocco's* most famous scene, she wears a pantsuit – the first time a female actor had done so in a Hollywood film – and kisses another woman on the lips.

While she could barely speak English when she appeared in the film, Dietrich's acting was nominated for an Academy Award, and she laid the groundwork for a star image that still resonates today.

Not surprisingly, Dietrich was as shocking off camera as she was in front of it. Having affairs with men *and* women – including some of her fellow actors – in the early 1930s was too scandalous to be widely reported, but in the decades that followed, she has become an icon for LGBT people, who were – and continue to be – inspired by her sexual independence.

SIMONE DE BEAUVOIR

JANUARY 9, 1908–APRIL 14, 1986

FRENCH

In her seminal work of militant feminism, *The Second Sex* (1949), Simone de Beauvoir claimed that although born equal to men, women are living as second-class citizens in the twentieth century, as social constraints and conditioning consign women to their inferior position. Prior to this theory, many believed women were *literally* born inferior to men. Her work is a cornerstone of feminist theory, which has not lost its power to shock, even today.

Born in Paris, the French novelist, philosopher, and critic Simone de Beauvoir studied at the Sorbonne, where she met her life-long lover and mentor, the philosopher Jean-Paul Sartre. Rejecting the conventional and religious ways of her lawyer father and devoutly Catholic mother, de Beauvoir eschewed traditional marriage and instead had several love affairs during her life, with both men and women.

During her profound affair with novelist Nelson Algren, it is claimed that she was at last able to achieve a highly charged, sexual orgasm, and this experience partially inspired her to write her ground breaking feminist treatise, *The Second Sex*. Confusingly, her complex personal life contradicted the militant feminist viewpoint she held in public and in her publications. De Beauvoir was an existentialist and therefore believed that "existence precedes essence." This belief, combined with her awareness of society's oppressive male hierarchy, would eventually result in her theory that "one is not born a woman, but becomes one."

Her argument that females are not born inferior to males may sound perfectly acceptable now but, prior to the publication of *The Second Sex*, it was widely believed that women were born inferior to men, and were even considered unstable deviants. De Beauvoir also argued that females should never view males as the absolute archetype of the human species toward which women should aspire. She was an active member of the French Women's Liberation Movement, and she is one of the famous women who, by claiming (falsely it transpired) to have had an abortion, forced the French government into legalizing abortion in 1974.

She should be highly regarded as the godmother of feminism and initiator of equality for women throughout Western society.

BETTY FRIEDAN

FEBRUARY 4, 1921–FEBRUARY 4, 2006

AMERICAN

Betty Friedan's publication of *The Feminine Mystique* signaled the beginning of the modern women's movement in the United States and helped to focus worldwide attention on women's rights.

In 1957, American author Betty Friedan was asked to develop and analyze responses to a survey of her classmates from prestigious Smith College. Like Friedan, most Smith graduates were middle-class, college-educated white women who had married and become mothers. Friedan discovered a common dissatisfaction among these women that was reflective of society, calling it the "problem that has no name."

In 1963, after intensive research, Friedan published her findings in *The Feminine Mystique*. To her surprise, Friedan found it was an instant bestseller. Although she blamed "women's magazines" and the advertising industry for perpetuating the image of women as satisfied with living vicariously through their husbands and children, leading women's publications ran excerpts from *The Feminine Mystique*.

Critics accused Friedan of trying to destroy the nuclear family and, while many males became ardent feminists, others felt threatened by the accusation that women were not always fulfilled by traditional roles. Since the passage of the women's suffrage amendment in 1920, the American women's movement had been dormant. Friedan's book galvanized women into action, and she became known as the Mother of the Second Wave of the women's movement. She co-founded the National Organization of Women (1966) and the National Women's Political Caucus (1971) to promote political and social goals of the movement.

Over succeeding decades, the women's movement influenced women around the world, lead to changing societal views on women's roles and abilities, and to the passage of laws prohibiting sexual discrimination.

⚜

QUEEN ELIZABETH II

APRIL 21, 1926

BRITISH

Queen Elizabeth is the longest-reigning British monarch, and her coronation marked the start of her rule during a period of great social and political change.

When Princess Elizabeth was born, on April 21, 1926, to the Duke and Duchess of York, it was never anticipated that she would become queen. Her father was the younger son of King George V and, therefore, his elder brother Edward was heir to the British throne. However, following George V's death in 1936, and Edward VIII's abdication that same year due to his intention to marry American divorcee Wallis Simpson, Elizabeth's father acceded to the throne, becoming King George VI.

As heir apparent, Princess Elizabeth married her distant cousin, Philip Mountbatten, formerly Prince Philip of Greece and Denmark, in 1947. Upon their marriage, he took the title Prince Philip, Duke of Edinburgh. Once married, they traveled widely, and it was while on one of their royal trips, visiting Kenya in February, 1952, that Princess Elizabeth received the devastating news that her beloved father had died of lung cancer. Now Queen Elizabeth, she immediately flew home to Britain. She was twenty-five years old.

Her coronation took place in Westminster Abbey on June 2, 1953, in front of more than 8,000 guests, including her son and heir Prince Charles, born in 1948. The streets of London were lined with an estimated three million people waiting to catch sight of the new monarch in the golden state coach. It was the first, and remains the only, British coronation to be broadcast on television and, while few families could afford a television set, those who could were able to watch the moving and ancient ceremony unfold.

Throughout her long reign, and three post-war generations, Queen Elizabeth II has been an integral part of the transformation from the old British Empire to the new British Commonweath and is widely accepted as a respected and stable head of state.

AUDREY HEPBURN

MAY 4, 1929–JANUARY 20, 1993

BRITISH

Actor, fashion icon, and philanthropist Audrey Hepburn burst onto the Broadway stage at the age of 22, setting new style standards in *Breakfast at Tiffany's*, became one of Hollywood's greatest icons, and, for several decades, dedicated her life to her humanitarian work for UNICEF.

Audrey Hepburn was born in Brussels, Belgium, the daughter of
J. A. Hepburn-Ruston and Baroness Ella van Heemstra. Her father, a
banker, left the family home when she was eight years old and she went
to England with her mother where she attended a private girls' school.
At the outbreak of World War II, the two of them traveled to Arnhem,
Netherlands, a neutral country, where her mother falsely believed
they'd be safe. It was here where Hepburn fell on hard times during the
Nazi occupation, suffering from depression and malnutrition.

After the liberation, Hepburn went to a ballet school in London on a
scholarship, but her height and the malnutrition she suffered during
the war meant that she was unable to pursue her dream of becoming a
great ballerina, so she decided to seek work as an actor. She soon found
success, and became a major Hollywood star of the 1950s and 1960s,
starring in such classic films as *Roman Holiday* (1953), *The Nun's Story*
(1959), and, most famously, *Breakfast at Tiffany's* (1961).

As an actor and one of Hollywood's greatest style icons, Audrey
Hepburn always dazzled with natural beauty and grace, but in the late
1980s acting took a back seat to her work as a goodwill ambassador
for UNICEF. The harrowing experiences of war had left a profound
mark on Hepburn, one reason for her dedicated commitment to the
children's charity.

In 1993, Hepburn won a special Academy Award for her humanitarian
work but, sadly, she did not live long enough to receive it. Her work to
help children on a global scale continues with a memorial fund set up
in her name.

JACQUELINE KENNEDY ONASSIS

JULY 28, 1929–MAY 19, 1994

AMERICAN

Jacqueline (Jackie) Kennedy Onassis was a most beloved and iconic American First Lady. She epitomized grace and elegance and became a global style icon.

Born in Southampton, New York, Onassis enjoyed a privileged childhood – her father was a New York stockbroker and her mother an accomplished equestrienne. She attended a prestigious boarding school in Connecticut, where she excelled, writing extensively for her school newspaper and winning an award for the school's top literature student in her senior year.

Onassis went on to Vassar College in New York to study history, literature, art, and French, spending her junior year in Paris. She then transferred to George Washington University in Washington, D.C., where she studied French literature. She graduated in 1951 and got a job with a local newspaper, the *Washington Times-Herald*. It was at a dinner party in 1952 where she met young congressman and senator-elect John F. Kennedy. They married two years later.

On November 8, 1960, Kennedy became president of the United States, and Onassis First Lady. She had campaigned tirelessly on Kennedy's behalf and she herself became a huge asset to the country – intelligent and cultured, charming and elegant, she won wide praise for her beauty, style, and facility with languages. It was through her role as First Lady that she established herself as a great patron for the arts and inspired patriotism through her restoration of the White House. Her strength and courage during some of the country's darkest periods, and her dignity throughout her own personal tragedies, has inspired a plethora of books and films about her.

In 1968, five years after JFK's shocking assassination, Onassis married Greek shipping magnate Aristotle Onassis. However, he died seven years later and Onassis became a widow for a second time. It is at this juncture that she returned to her love of writing and became an editor at Viking Press and then Doubleday, spanning a late, but successful, 20-year career. However, she will always be remembered for her time as America's First Lady and the profound effect she had on U.S. society and the world beyond.

❦

MARY QUANT

FEBRUARY 11, 1934

BRITISH

A British fashion icon and trendsetter, Mary
Quant's introduction of the mini skirt – regarded
with outrage by some when it first appeared –
became the defining image of "Swinging London"
in the 1960s and revolutionizing the
fashion industry.

There is some disagreement over who originally designed the mini skirt, though it is generally considered to be the French designer André Courrèges. Another contender is John Bates, who designed the clothes for Diana Rigg in *The Avengers* television series. Without a doubt, however, it was Mary Quant who popularized mini skirts when she started producing them in 1960 for her King's Road boutique, Bazaar, in London's fashionable Chelsea.

Born in 1934, Quant gained a diploma in art education at Goldsmith's College, London, and opened her boutique in 1957 with her husband Alexander Plunket Greene. Her range of clothing was uniquely aimed at teenagers and young adults, and was known for its innovative geometric and colorful designs. Previous designers had been unable to get stores to accept a skirt with a hemline above the knee but, as Quant had her own shop, she had no difficulties selling her even shorter version to the trendsetting Chelsea Set.

Usually around seven inches above the knee, the skirt did not become widely worn until 1966, but it soon became a symbol of "Swinging London" and was known as the "Chelsea Look." Its popularity also increased sales of the new replacement for stockings known as tights, and Mary Quant was soon designing tights in different colors to add to the look.

An icon of 1960s fashion, Mary Quant was awarded an OBE in 1966 for her services to the fashion industry, and later designed hot pants as well as a range of make-up.

GERMAINE GREER

JANUARY 29, 1939

AUSTRALIAN

Germaine Greer's The Female Eunuch is a feminist classic that gave voice to the discontent and demands driving an emerging social movement. Deliberately subversive and polemic in style and message, *The Female Eunuch* is an affront against the pillars of Western patriarchal society, ranging from religion to ideals of feminine beauty.

A classic of Second Wave feminism and an international bestseller, *The Female Eunuch* caused a furore when it was first published in 1970. Angry and revolutionary in tone, Germaine Greer scrutinizes the myth of female inferiority by taking apart supposedly scientific theories of gender difference. The book demonstrates how women are trained from an early age to be sexually passive, arguing that this repression of sexual desire and curiosity turns women into "female eunuchs."

Greer challenges women to reject negative body images, to rediscover their libido, and to let go of their confining role in the nuclear family. *The Female Eunuch* pairs its attack on patriarchy with a critique of capitalism, suggesting that consumerism contributes to female entrapment.

Some may be surprised that Greer's feminist classic ends with a conciliatory note toward the other sex, indicating that women's struggle for emancipation could serve as an inspiration for men once "they jumped off their own treadmill." Although the position of women in Western society has undergone significant changes since the publication of *The Female Eunuch*, Greer's irreverent musings about the pressures surrounding body hair and curves, and the roots of gender inequality have not become irrelevant.

The Female Eunuch continues to divide its readers and remains a living testimony to the social movement of feminism that many would have liked to declare dead long ago.

ALICE WALKER

FEBRUARY 9, 1944

AMERICAN

Alice Walker became the first African-American woman to receive the Pulitzer Prize, for her best-selling novel, *The Color Purple*.

On its publication in 1982, *The Color Purple* immediately found itself both a bestseller and a highly controversial talking point. There were many who attacked Alice Walker's book, claiming it showed age-old stereotypes of violent, stupid, and abusive black masculinity. For many readers, though, this was one of the most life-affirming and empowering novels of the late twentieth century.

It tells the story of Celie, a young, uneducated, black American girl raped by her stepfather, and then sold to her husband who deprives her of her beloved sister, Nettie. Ironically, it is when her husband brings his mistress, Shug, home to live with them, that Celie's life is transformed. She is fascinated by Shug, a beautiful, glamorous singer who commands attention and expects adoration. The two women become lovers and, with Shug's support, Celie finds the strength to leave her husband and begin an independent life.

Celie's story is entwined with that of other women – her friend, Squeak, her long-lost sister, Nettie, and the powerfully built Sophie, who is sent to prison for knocking a white man to the pavement. Celie is doubly abused, firstly for her color and then for her gender.

Yet the quality that made this book a bestseller was the tenderness of the writing. It's written in the form of letters, giving the story directness and a distinctive voice, and Alice Walker infuses the black folk English with a lyric quality. The novel captured the harshness of early-twentieth-century black American rural life, as well as offering one of the most welcome happy endings ever.

CAITLYN JENNER

OCTOBER 28, 1949

AMERICAN

Caitlyn Jenner is a well-known television personality and was, as Bruce Jenner, one of the most beloved athletes of the 1970s. It was when Jenner announced on Twitter that she is a woman – now known as Caitlyn – that she set the world on fire, becoming an instant transgender icon.

Jenner was born in Mount Kisco, New York, and struggled at school due to dyslexia, but excelled at sports, track and field in particular, and went on to achieve Olympic stardom. Then, after years out of the spotlight, Jenner worked on several television series and starred in TV films, but in recent years has become most famous for appearing in the reality series *Keeping Up With the Kardashians*, with then wife Kris Jenner, children Kendall and Kylie Jenner, and stepchildren Robert Jr., Kim, Kourtney and Khloé Kardashian.

In April 2015, after much tabloid press speculation, Jenner appeared in an exclusive TV interview with Diane Sawyer, in which she announced that she identified as a woman. Then on June 1, the world was introduced to Caitlyn via Twitter, through a tweet in which Jenner announced, "I'm so happy after such a long struggle to be living my true self. Welcome to the world Caitlyn."

On the same day she featured on the cover of *Vanity Fair* and, later that year, *Glamour* magazine named her one of its 25 Glamour Women of the Year, branding her a "Trans Champion."

Jenner has since used her prominence as the world's most famous openly transgender woman to speak out about tolerance of people's differences, and has inspired transgender people all over the world to reveal their true identities.

OPRAH WINFREY

JANUARY 29, 1954

AMERICAN

Oprah Winfrey became the first African-American woman to host a successful national daytime talk show, and has gone on to become one of the most powerful African-Americans in the twenty-first century.

After a poor and troubled childhood, Oprah Winfrey began her broadcasting career while still in high school, at WVOL radio in Nashville. At nineteen, she became the youngest (and first African-American) woman to report the news at Nashville's WTVF-TV and later moved to Baltimore to host a local talk show.

However, Winfrey's success truly began when she moved to Chicago in 1984 to host the morning talk show, *AM Chicago*, which became the number-one local show only a month after her arrival. Just two years later, the show expanded to an hour in length and entered into national syndication, renamed as *The Oprah Winfrey Show*.

The Oprah Winfrey Show became one of the most successful talk shows in the nation. Though it started out by reporting sensational stories, Oprah's talk show shifted to therapeutic topics, emphasizing emotional healing and self-fulfilment. This evolution was reflected in 1998 when *The Oprah Winfrey Show* won the National Academy of Television Arts & Sciences Lifetime Achievement Award. Winfrey went on to introduce a successful magazine, called, *O, The Oprah Magazine*, and set up her own production company, Harpo Productions, Inc.

But while Winfrey is an iconic figure in television, she is equally lauded for her philanthropy. With a strong belief in education, she has contributed millions of dollars to organizations around the world. Once described by *Time* magazine as one of the most influential people of the twenty-first century, Oprah Winfrey is a success story that will continue to inspire in generations to come.

❦

DIANA, PRINCESS OF WALES

JULY 1, 1961–31 AUGUST 31, 1997

BRITISH

Best-known for her caring, open nature and her humanitarian, charitable acts, Diana, Princess of Wales brought a further humility to the British Royal Family and will be remembered as the "Queen of Peoples' Hearts".

Diana Spencer was the fourth of five children born to John Spencer and his first wife, Frances. A family of British nobility, she grew up in Park House on the Sandringham estate. Although she did not excel academically, she was complimented for her talent in such activities as swimming and dance, and for her great community spirit – a quality that would prove to serve her well, and help her overcome her perceived shyness, in her future public appearances as Princess.

Although meeting several times before, it was from the summer of 1980 that Prince Charles and Lady Diana started courting, and the prospect of their future marriage became a high possibility. After being well received by the Queen, Charles proposed to Diana on February 6, 1981, and their "fairytale wedding" at St Paul's Cathedral in London took place in front of an audience of over 750 million people worldwide. This union made Diana the Princess of Wales – the third-highest ranking female in the United Kingdom Order of Precedence.

Despite an open struggle with her new public role, Princess Diana immersed herself in charitable works, making 397 official engagements in 1991 alone. These involved visiting Great Ormond Street Hospital, of which she became president, and, controversially at the time, supporting HIV and AIDS charities. It was her physical contact with these victims for which she is well known, and she was a key figure who helped fight its stigma. During her visit to South Africa in 1997, President Nelson Mandela championed her for having "transformed public attitude and improved the chances of such people."

Despite the happy welcome of their two sons, Princes William and Harry, Princess Diana's troubled marriage soon became public speculation, and divorce was confirmed in 1996. Sadly, just one year later, tragedy followed on August 31, 1997, when Princess Diana was killed in a car crash in Paris. This news shook not only her family but the whole world. The "People's Princess" legacy not only continues in her work but with her children, who further her charitable efforts and compassion.

SHERYL SANDBERG

AUGUST 28, 1969

AMERICAN

Sheryl Sandberg is an outspoken advocate for women in business, the COO of Facebook and best-selling author of *Lean-In: Women, Work, and the Will to Lead.*

Sheryl Sandberg was born in Washington, D.C. but moved to North Miami Beach, Florida, at the age of two. She later majored in economics at Harvard, and while studying there, co-founded a group called Women in Economics and Government, created "to get more women to major in government and economics."

She then attained an MBA from Harvard Business School, graduating in 1995, and embarked on a career within government as a research assistant and then chief of staff to the then Deputy Treasury Secretary, Lawrence Summers.

Sandberg's next stop was Silicon Valley, where she joined the "tech boom" gang, first with Google, where she became vice president of global online sales and operations, and gained a formidable reputation as one of the country's top business executives. In 2008, Sandberg became Facebook's COO and, in 2014, made it onto the billionaires' list.

Sandberg has become a zealous advocate for women in the workplace, encouraging women to be more aggressive in seeking success within the business world. Her book *Lean In: Women, Work, and the Will to Lead* (2013) has sold over a million copies and inspired the community-building group LeanIn.org, founded by Sandberg to support women striving to meet their ambitions.

❦

AUDREY PULVAR

FEBRUARY 21, 1972

FRENCH

In 2004, Audrey Pulvar became the first black newsreader to present the main evening news on national television in France. Before Pulvar, black news reporters had only been seen on French television in weather forecasts or regional news.

Black citizens in France had long suffered underrepresentation in the French media. While non-European immigrants constituted approximately 15 per cent of the French population, they were more vulnerable to poverty and unemployment than their white counterparts, and were regarded as an "invisible" social group. Efforts to promote the visibility of minorities were not wholeheartedly embraced, partly due to the French ideal of equality regardless of race or religion, which thwarted affirmative action.

But by the turn of the millennium, voices were gradually being raised. In 1998, 40,000 black people marched in Paris to commemorate the 150th anniversary of the end of slavery, and France won the soccer World Cup with a team with many black players. In early 2004, the High Council on Integration demanded that the government make it a condition of every broadcast channel to ensure immigrants are "fairly and properly represented."

Born in 1972, on Martinique, a Caribbean island, Audrey Pulvar worked for a Martinique TV channel before moving to a Caribbean network. In 2002, she was hired by state-funded company France Televisions, and in the following year appeared onscreen to report regional news. In September 2004, as part of the company's "positive action integration plan," Pulvar, aged thirty-two, became the first black newsreader to present the main evening news on national television in France.

The editor of France 3's national news programs, Ulysse Gosset, claimed he hoped it would spark "a small revolution" in the world of French TV.

CHIMAMANDA NGOZI ADICHIE

SEPTEMBER 15, 1977

NIGERIAN

Through her words, both written and spoken, prize-winning novelist and feminist campaigner Chimamanda Ngozi Adichie has confronted race and gender issues and challenged ingrained prejudices.

Chimamanda Ngozi Adichie was born in Enugu, Nigeria to a middle-class Igbo family. Her mother became the first female registrar at the University of Nigeria, while her father was a professor of statistics there. Under pressure to do what was expected of her, Adichie went on to study medicine at the University of Nigeria, but she left after a year and a half to pursue her ambition to become a writer, taking up a scholarship and moving to the U.S., where she studied communication and political science at Eastern Connecticut State University.

It was during her senior year at Eastern that she started working on her first novel, *Purple Hibiscus* (2003). It was shortlisted for the Orange Fiction Prize (2004) and was awarded the Commonwealth Writers' Prize for Best First Book (2005). Her other novels, *Half of a Yellow Sun* (2006)and *Americanah* (2009), along with her short stories, are also widely critically acclaimed.

Through her works, Adichie tries to combat the image of Africans as portrayed by Western media and she has been credited with attracting a new generation of readers to African literature. Alongside her numerous literary nominations and awards, Adichie was listed, in 2015, in *Time* magazine's "The 100 Most Influential People."

Her rousing text *We Should All be Feminists* is one of her most important. Based on an inspiring TEDx talk she gave in 2012 (Pop diva Beyoncé was so inspired by Adichie's speech that she sampled it in her 2013 track "***Flawless"), this book-length essay offers a unique and brilliantly presented definition of feminism for the 21st century and initiated a global conversation on the subject. This is a remarkable exploration and a rallying cry of what it's like to be a woman in the 21st century.

THE ARTS

Mary Cassatt

Beatrix Potter

Isadora Duncan

Vanessa Bell

Virginia Woolf

Georgia O'Keeffe

Agatha Christie

Hattie McDaniel

Leni Riefenstahl

Daphne du Maurier

Frida Kahlo

Amrita Sher-Gil

Maya Angelou

Toni Morrison

Sylvia Plath

Margaret Atwood

Tracey Emin

J. K. Rowling

MARY CASSATT

MAY 22, 1844–JUNE 14, 1926

AMERICAN

In 1900, Mary Cassatt was using her considerable influence to advise American collectors to buy French Impressionist works of art. Many Impressionist works were bequeathed to the newly formed museums in America's principal cities. Thus, Cassatt helped to introduce avant-garde art to America.

Mary Cassatt was born in Allegheny City, Pennsylvania, into a wealthy family and enjoyed a well-traveled youth. She studied at the Pennsylvania Academy of Fine Arts from 1861 to 1865 but was disillusioned by the conservative teaching there and went to Paris, where she attended private classes. She studied the work of the Old Masters during extensive travels in Europe.

She settled in Paris, in 1874, and saw Degas' work the following year. Through her productive alliance with Degas, and her understanding of avant-garde ideas, she produced innovative paintings of bourgeois domesticity and leisure which demonstrate an economic draftsmanship and a vigorous handling of paint.

Her articulations of asymmetric compositional devices demonstrate her appreciation of Japanese printmaking. This was further developed by her visit to a Japanese print exhibition in 1890, after which she produced a series of inventive prints. By the 1890s, she was pursuing these ideas in the spatial structures of her paintings, culminating in *The Boating Party* (1893–94), where she skilfully used flattened planes of color to focus attention on the central figure of a child.

Some of her most intriguing paintings are those of women with children. These paintings demonstrate her use of ingenious formal methods to show the physical bond between mother and child. Cassatt succeeded in a predominantly male profession, at a time when women's choices were circumscribed by late-nineteenth-century conventions.

BEATRIX POTTER

JULY 28, 1866–DECEMBER 22, 1943

ENGLISH

A writer, illustrator, and conservationist, Beatrix Potter's immediate best-seller, *The Tale of Peter Rabbit*, was the first of thirty or so tales that Beatrix Potter wrote for Frederick Warne & Co. Peter and co. can still be seen in nursery rooms around the world today.

When Peter Rabbit hopped into the middle-class nursery and took up residence there, it changed very young children's reading forever. *The Tale of Peter Rabbit* was the first of what Beatrix Potter called her "little books." These exquisitely illustrated narratives, by Potter herself, which tell the adventures of a whole host of English farm and country animals, would become one of the most popular series of children's literature of all time.

Potter was an experienced naturalist and the figure of her hero is anatomically exact, from the way he hops to the way he hides. All the same, Peter is elevated from mere bunnyhood by his blue coat, a garment that in time became almost as famous as its wearer. The garden setting, too, recognisably belongs to the cottage plots of Potter's beloved Lancashire. It is the story, however, that elevates *The Tale of Peter Rabbit* from being simply a charming picture book for children learning to read. Spare and elegant, it fuses rabbit psychology with that of a small child. It is Peter's curiosity, and his insistence on doing precisely what his mother tells him not to do, that makes him such a delightfully sympathetic hero for any young reader.

It was from Potter's holidays in Scotland and the Lake District that developed her love of nature, of which she closely observed, painted, and, later, preserved. Following the success of her "little books," she began to purchase properties – consisting of farms and their houses – in and around the Lake District. Making them working farms, Potter was responsible for the up-keep and restoration of many farms that may have otherwise been left empty. It is this wealth of property that is preserved, and can be visited today, due to her leaving almost all of it to the Lake District National Park, following her death in 1943.

Today, as well as her legacy of being a prolific and much-loved children's writer, she truly is an ambassador for nature and conservation.

ISADORA DUNCAN

MAY 26, 1877–SEPTEMBER 14, 1927

AMERICAN

Isadora Duncan pioneered the modern dance movement when she abandoned traditional ballet for a more expressive, emotional style that is danced barefoot.

American dancer Isadora Duncan is often known as the "mother of modern dance." Wearing loose flowing, seductive tunics while dancing barefoot, she rejected the conventions of traditional schools of ballet and dance to develop her own philosophy based on the writings of German philosopher Friedrich Nietzsche. Duncan applauded Nietzsche's focus on creativity and health, and his belief in affirming the realities of real life rather than the afterlife.

In 1903, Duncan delivered a speech in Berlin called "The Dance of the Future." Here she outlined her philosophy of dance, stating that it should be more like that of the ancient Greeks, emphasizing natural movements and rhythms to express both human forms and emotions. Though initially received with critical reviews in America, by 1909, Duncan was internationally acclaimed for her dance performances and choreography.

Duncan founded three dance schools for girls based on her philosophy, in France, Germany, and Russia. Preferring simple scenery and costumes over elaborate ones, she maintained that the dancer should be the focus of attention, and was the first to suggest that dance deserves a place among the high arts.

Duncan also became known for her exciting, unconventional, and tragic personal life. This included scandalous romances, the accidental death of both of her children, frequent public drunkenness, and financial troubles. In 1927, Duncan was tragically killed when one of her famous long scarves became entangled in the wheel of her motorcycle.

VANESSA BELL

MAY 30, 1879–APRIL 7, 1961

ENGLISH

Vanessa Bell was the sister of writer Virginia Woolf and member of the "modern thing" Bloomsbury Group. Bell's shared creativity led her to become a leading figure in the development of British modernist painting.

Vanessa Bell (born Vanessa Stephen) was one of the leading exponents of British Post-Impressionism. The eldest daughter of the eminent man of letters Sir Leslie Stephen and his second wife Julia Duckworth, she was born into the Victorian "intellectual aristocracy." As children she and her sister decided their respective destinies: she would be a painter and Virginia (later Virginia Woolf) would be a writer.

Bell married the writer and art critic Clive Bell; their house at 46 Gordon Square became the headquarters of the Bloomsbury Group. Bell's art was transformed by her response to Roger Fry's two Post-Impressionist exhibitions of 1910 and 1912. Under the influence of Matisse in particular, her style was characterized by radically simplified and flattened forms – most effectively articulated in works such as *Studland Beach* (c.1912) – and by a dazzling use of color, brilliantly illustrated by her portrait of Mary Hutchinson, *Mrs St. John Hutchinson.* (1915).

Around 1914, Bell produced some of the first purely non-representational paintings in Britain. Her flirtation with abstraction was short-lived, however, and for the remainder of her career she concentrated on still life, landscape, and domestic subjects.

From 1913 to the end of her life, Bell lived with, and frequently worked alongside, Duncan Grant. She and Grant collaborated on many schemes of interior decoration, but their individual idioms remained distinct: his exuberant, lyrical, fantastic; hers self-effacing, grave, even severe. Much of her early work was destroyed during the Blitz, but what survives confirms her contribution to early British modernism.

❦

VIRGINIA WOOLF

JANUARY 25, 1882–MARCH 28, 1941

ENGLISH

Virginia Woolf's experimental use of the narrative form paved the way for many of the more extreme expressions of the postmodernist period. In the words of E. M. Forster, she pushed the English language "a little further against the dark."

In popular literary consciousness, Virginia Woolf is most famous for developing a style of writing known as "stream of consciousness." Her later detractors in the post-war period characterized this apparently formless interior narrative as the indulgent twittering of a privileged novelist who had few real concerns – poverty, hunger – to write about. From the 1970s, however, a new generation of literary critics and feminist scholars insisted on seeing Woolf as a key modernist whose pioneering novels and essays challenged traditional forms of narrative in both fiction and biography.

In 1904, Virginia and her sister Vanessa moved from Kensington to Gordon Square. There they came to know the loose-knit circle of writers and painters known as the Bloomsbury Group. One of these – the writer and political activist Leonard Woolf – later became Virginia's husband and nursed her through escalating bouts of mental illness.

In novels such as *Night and Day* (1919), *Mrs. Dalloway* (1925), and *To The Lighthouse* (1927), Woolf eschews plot-driven narrative in favour of exploring her characters' inner consciousness. The result is an intense lyricism, preoccupied with auditory and visual sensation rather than the record of mere events. Meanwhile, in cod-biographies such as *Orlando* (1928) and *Flush* (1933), Woolf attempts this same approach with apparently non-fictional subjects.

For a generation raised on the solid realism of Victorian novel and biography, this amounted to revolution or desecration, depending on your point of view. In March 1941, depressed by the way the war was going (if the Germans invaded, the Woolfs would almost certainly become a key target), Virginia Woolf drowned herself by weighting her pockets with stones and walking into the river near her Sussex home. Yet, to this day, she is considered one of the most significant modernist authors of the 20th century – a pioneer in stream-of-consciousness writing.

GEORGIA O'KEEFFE

NOVEMBER 15, 1887–MARCH 6, 1986

AMERICAN

In her largescale flower paintings, Georgia O'Keeffe created representational art that at the same time appeared abstract, making her a reputation as the most important female artist in the United States and the "Mother of American modernism."

Born in Sun Prairie, Wisconsin, O'Keeffe studied at the Art Institute of Chicago in 1904, and at the Art Students' League of New York three years later. She taught art in Texas from 1913 to 1918. In 1916, American photographer and art gallery director Alfred Stieglitz – with whom O'Keeffe was romantically linked and later married – showed an interest in her abstract drawings. That same year, he exhibited them in his famous gallery in New York, the 291, marking a turning point in her career.

In 1923, Stieglitz held a major exhibit of O'Keeffe's work at the Anderson Galleries, the first of many of her showings. The following year, she painted a large-scale flower, *Petunia No 2*, in a style that would become her hallmark. The details of the flower are so enlarged that they become unfamiliar and abstract. In 1929, Beck Strand, a friend and fellow modernist, invited O'Keeffe to New Mexico, where she found new inspiration for her large-scale paintings. She started collecting and painting bones, and two years later painted *Cow's Skull: Red, White and Blue*.

In 1931, she suffered a nervous breakdown, and, in 1949, three years after Stieglitz's death, moved permanently to New Mexico, where she met fellow artists Frida Kahlo and Miguel Covarrubias in 1951. In the 1960s, inspired by aircraft flights, she introduced elements of the sky and clouds into her paintings. One of her largest works was *Sky above Clouds* (1965). She died aged ninety-eight in Santa Fe.

Following her death, The Georgia O'Keeffe Museum was established, and is still open, in Santa Fe. As a tribute to her life's work, it holds 140 of O'Keeffe's oil paintings, nearly 700 drawings, and hundreds of additional works from her life. One of the most significant female artists of the 20th century, Georgia O'Keeffe was committed to creating imagery that portrayed what she called "the wideness and wonder of the world as I live in it."

❦

AGATHA CHRISTIE

SEPTEMBER 15, 1890–JANUARY 12, 1976

ENGLISH

Claimed in Guiness World Records lists as the best-selling novelist of all time, Agatha Christie's storytelling, comprising of 66 detective novels and 14 short stories, provided the archetype for the modern crime novel.

Initially an unsuccessful writer with six rejections, Agatha Christie is best-known today for the eerily engaging whodunit mystery novels such as *Murder on the Orient Express*. Christie's ongoing character, the detective Hercule Poirot, starred in her first novel, *The Mysterious Affair at Styles*, published in 1920. Drawing on a tradition put forth by Arthur Conan Doyle with his *Sherlock Holmes* stories, Christie followed Poirot through many adventures over the years, building up a personality marked by keen investigatory skills.

The British author created situations littered with clues leading up to conclusive finishes. In *The Mysterious Affair at Styles*, she laid out the framework: several people drawn together at an isolated manor, all of whom suspects in a murder, and letting Poirot put everything together at the end. This classic structure came to define the golden age of detective fiction.

In keeping with the mystery of her novels, Christie is known for her own disappearance in 1926. After 11 days, Christie was discovered living quietly in a hotel in Yorkshire. She appeared to have no recollection of her real identity, nor of the events of the past few days. Doctors said she was suffering from amnesia brought about by the death of her mother. In fact, a definitive explanation is still wanting. Some people thought that it must be a stunt to boost sales of her latest book, but far more likely is the theory that Christie was distraught over the affair of her husband with another woman. Whether Christie consciously staged her disappearance, or was suffering from a "fugue state," is something which continues to fascinate.

Yet Christie's career in writing flourished, sitting her at the top of many literary triumphs. Her famous work, *And Then There Were None*, has sold over 100 million copies worldwide and is consequently one of the best-selling books of all time. Her stage play *The Mousetrap* holds the world record for its longest initial run, and she remains the most-translated author, having been translated into over 100 languages.

HATTIE MCDANIEL

JUNE 10, 1895–OCTOBER 26, 1952

AMERICAN

By winning an Oscar in 1940 for her role in
Gone With the Wind, Hattie McDaniel proved
at the time that African-American actors were as
talented as white actors, worthy of recognition,
even though they were restricted to secondary
roles in Hollywood films.

Despite their many contributions to the arts in the first half of the twentieth century, African-Americans found little success in mainstream motion pictures, where they experienced systematic racism and discrimination. In many Hollywood films, African-Americans only appeared in secondary roles – servants, cooks, porters, maids, and shoe shiners – and were paid less for their work than their white counterparts.

Moreover, movie theaters were often segregated in this period, particularly in the South. If filmmakers wanted to utilize black actors in roles that better reflected the African-American experience, they could only produce so-called "race films," movies created for an all-black audience.

Given this, it is not surprising that Hattie McDaniel's role as a maid in *Gone With The Wind*, and her subsequent Oscar win, had a mixed reception by black audiences. McDaniel's best-known line from the film, "I don't know nothing about birthing babies," was derided by many African-Americans, who saw the phrase as emblematic of the patronizing way black people were treated by Hollywood. However, some African-Americans regarded McDaniel's victory as a source of pride, despite their problems with the role itself.

Today, McDaniel is viewed as both a symbol of the way Hollywood treated African-Americans before the civil-rights movement of the 1960s, and a pioneer for the African-American actors that followed her.

LENI RIEFENSTAHL

AUGUST 22, 1902–SEPTEMBER 8, 2003

GERMAN

Together with her most talked about film, *Olympia*, Leni Riefenstahl was a film director, producer, and screenwriter with a controversial tour de force that combined technical innovation with questionable political motives.

Leni Riefenstahl's *Olympia* has been both celebrated and condemned in equal measure. For her technical innovations in shooting live action at the 1936 Olympic Games in Berlin, and not least the poetry of her editing technique that makes *Olympia* so enthralling, Riefenstahl is justly celebrated as one of cinema history's most important filmmakers.

That she willingly deployed her skills to promote Nazism on such a captivating scale, and that she failed to accept any moral responsibility for her role in doing so, also led, however, to her being repeatedly castigated throughout her life. That said, *Olympia* is a tour de force that is justly studied as a key work of twentieth-century cinema.

The film was produced in two parts: *Festival of Peoples* (*Fest der Völker*) and *Festival of Beauty* (*Fest der Schönheit*), but multiple versions exist due to the director's habit of re-editing for each re-release. Although many of the film's techniques are now industry standard (for example, the diversity of camera angles, smash-cut and jump-cut editing techniques, extreme close-ups, and remote camera tracking shots), and Riefenstahl's place as an innovator equal to Abel Gance (1889–1981) and Sergei Eisenstein (1898–1948) is thus assured, praise for the film and Riefenstahl's overall aesthetic has often drawn condemnation.

For this reason, Riefenstahl remains one of the most controversial figures in the history of cinema, with opinion still divided on whether *Olympia* is a film about the Olympic Games or a work of Nazi propaganda.

DAPHNE DU MAURIER

MAY 13, 1907–APRIL 19, 1989

ENGLISH

Daphne du Maurier was one of the 20th century's most successful writers of popular novels and period novels of sensation. Although initially considered as a romantic novelist, her works are far more in the Gothic genre due to their moody, dark, and sometimes paranormal overtones.

Daphne du Maurier was one of the bestselling novelists of the early and mid-twentieth century, and her later influence encompasses film, thriller writing, and historical fiction. She came from a cultured family – her father was a successful actor-manager, and her grandfather a famous novelist (George du Maurier, author of *Trilby*). She was a master of suspense and sensation, with a virtuosic understanding of the psychology of fear.

Rebecca (1938) is generally taken to be her masterpiece, a dark romantic novel of intrigue and horrible passion. It recounts the tale of an innocent (never named) who finds it difficult to shake off the ghost of her new husband's first wife (Rebecca). The moral ambiguity of the novel demonstrates du Maurier's complexity and challenge to genre – whilst *Rebecca* ends (probably) happily, the couple are compromised by murder, arson, and jealousy.

The book is indebted to the work of the Bröntes (in later life, she wrote a biography of Branwell Brönte). *Rebecca*'s success made du Maurier one of the most famous and read writers in the world. Further thrillers set in Cornwall were lean, sharp pieces of writing. The narrative drive of her writing led to her work being successfully adapted for the cinema, including famous films of *Rebecca* and the short stories "Don't Look Now" (1973) and "The Birds" (1963).

These three key works demonstrate the eeriness and almost Gothic nature of her writing; certainly the threat of the unknown and repressed anxieties figure highly in her work, emphasized by the often reclusiveness of the works' settings in Cornwall, where she spent most of her life.

❧

FRIDA KAHLO

JULY 6, 1907–JULY 13, 1954

MEXICAN

Considered one of Mexico's greatest artists, Frida Kahlo was a rebellious individualist who became an icon of female creativity.

Frida Kahlo was born Magdalena Carmen Frieda Kahlo y Calderón, in Coyoacán, Mexico City. Her life was marked by physical suffering, starting with the polio she contracted at the age of five and worsening by the life-changing bus accident that caused severe injuries owing to a pole that pierced her from stomach to pelvis. The medicine of her time resulted in her body being tortured with multiple surgical operations (32 throughout her life), corsets of different kinds and archaic stretching machines.

She began painting during her recovery and finished her first self-portrait the following year. The physical pain she endured resonated throughout her paintings, mostly uncompromising self-portraits exploring, among many other things, the theme of identity. The language of suffering and symbolism of pain present in her work had not previously been explored by female artists and Kahlo made it legitimate for women to openly express their suffering. She dissected the impact of motherhood on female identity and articulated her feelings about her own miscarriages through several of her paintings.

Her personal life was as colorful and vibrant as her works and she is famed for her tumultuous relationship with muralist Diego Rivera (married 1929, divorced 1939, remarried 1940), her many love affairs, her heavy drinking, and her political activism (she was a member of the Mexican Communist Party), as well as for her striking artistic endeavours.

Kahlo has attracted popular interest to the extent that the term "Fridamania" was coined to describe the phenomenon, and in 2018, she was celebrated in the form of a Barbie doll, launched in celebration of International Women's Day. Rather controversially, her famous monobrow was missing – Kahlo's individualist aesthetics proving, it seems, too unconventional for the likes of Mattel.

❦

AMRITA SHER-GIL

JANUARY 30, 1913–DECEMBER 5, 1941

HUNGARIAN-INDIAN

Amrita Sher-Gil was the pioneer voice of modern
art in India, linking its ancestral artistic tradition
to modern social and political concerns.

Born into a family of intellectuals, with a Hungarian singer mother and an Indian scholar father, Amrita Sher-Gil grew up between Hungary and India. At the age of 16, she moved to Paris to study at the École nationale supérieure des Beaux-Arts, where she was taught a very academic approach to painting. But her stay in France also allowed her to discover Gauguin and his vivid depiction of the female body.

Leaving her exuberant lifestyle and her numerous lovers in France, she returned to India in 1934, where her work was influenced by the observation of people's daily lives. While her paintings initially retained the monumental sense of composition that she learnt in Paris, the facial expressions of her subjects reflect the artist's empathy. Her painting *Three Girls* (1935) dates from this period.

A year later, she met the collector Karl Khandalavala, who encouraged her to further her study of Indian artistic tradition, especially Moghul miniatures. At that point, Sher-Gil simplified her lines, and depurated the background to focus on the characters, which she depicted in colorful hues. As her sense of composition grew simpler, Sher-Gil developed a more complex political and social agenda. She became very concerned by the isolated fate of women dwelling in rural areas.

The expressive strength of her brushstrokes resides in the deep, melancholic gaze of her protagonists, reflecting a sense of silent suffering. Shortly after moving to the artistic town of Lahore, Sher-Gil suddenly died, aged just 28, in still unexplained circumstances.

MAYA ANGELOU

APRIL 4, 1928–MAY 28, 2014

AMERICAN

The great triumph of Maya Angelou's work was to break out of the ghetto of African-American liberationist writing and become a mainstream read. Her narrative of triumph over a sequence of tragedies spoke not just to black readers but to white women and gay men and women, all of whom were questioning their identity from the 1960s onwards.

Maya Angelou's six volumes of memoir and many works of poetry have made her one of the founding mothers of black literary consciousness in post-war America. *I Know Why the Caged Bird Sings*, which was first published in 1969, spent over two years on the *New York Times'* bestseller list and is now a permanent fixture on school and university syllabi on both sides of the Atlantic.

"Dr Angelou," as she liked to be known, was given many honorary degrees and a lifetime chair at Wake Forest University. In *The Caged Bird*, Angelou tells of a dirt-poor pre-war childhood spent with her grandmother in Arkansas. Angelou's style is lyrical, as lush as the steaming beauty of the southern landscape it describes. Later, the mood darkens as Angelou tells of her move to the city and rape at the hands of her mother's boyfriend.

When the man is lynched by outraged relatives, the seven-year-old Angelou refuses to speak for several years on the grounds that "I thought my voice had killed him." In later volumes of memoir, Angelou recounts her work as a cabaret artist as well as her involvement in the civil-rights movement and an extended stay in Ghana, searching for her spiritual homeland. Her intensely expressive and highly personal narratives struck a chord with all those people – especially African-Americans – who were struggling with issues of gender, race, and nationality in the 1970s and 1980s.

Up until her death, Angelou continued to be a national institution. In 1993, she was invited to read her work at President Clinton's inauguration, only the second poet to have had such an honor.

❧

TONI MORRISON

FEBRUARY 18, 1931

AMERICAN

A novelist, essayist, and professor emeritus, Toni Morrison's novel, *Beloved*, was named in the *New York Times Book Review* 2006, as the best American novel published in the last 25 years.

Toni Morrison, one of the most celebrated writers of our time, was born Chloe Anthony Wofford, on February 18, 1931, in Lorain, Ohio. Morrison earned a degree in English and classics from Howard University, and received her Master's from Cornell University, where she wrote her thesis on the literary works of Virginia Woolf and William Faulkner.

After graduation, Morrison taught literature at several universities and worked as an editor at Random House, before making her literary debut in 1970. *The Bluest Eye* (1970), Morrison's first novel, tells the story of Pecola Breedlove, a young black girl growing up in Lorain, Ohio. The story, told from five perspectives (Pecola's, her mother's, her father's, her friend Claudia's, and Soaphead Church's), deals with themes of identity, child molestation, and racism. Subsequently, Morrison published the novels *Sula* (1973), *Song of Solomon* (1977), *Beloved* (1987), *Jazz* (1992), and *Paradise* (1997).

When asked who she wrote for, during a lecture at Princeton University, where she holds the Robert F. Goheen Professorship in the Humanities, Morrison replied, "I want to write for people like me, which is to say, black people, curious people, demanding people – people who can't be faked, people who don't need to be patronized, people who have very, very high criteria."

Morrison's literary career has been marked with honors, including the National Book Critics Circle Award, the American Academy and Institute of Arts and Letters Award, the Pulitzer Prize, and the Robert F. Kennedy Award. In 1993, Morrison was the first African-American woman to be awarded the Nobel Prize in Literature.

❦

SYLVIA PLATH

OCTOBER 27, 1932–FEBRUARY 11, 1963

AMERICAN

Due to both the intensity of her imagery and the nature of her death, Sylvia Plath is one of the most iconic poets of the twentieth century.

Born in Massachusetts, Sylvia Plath showed literary promise at an early age when she published her first poem at just eight years old. After gaining a scholarship to Smith College, where she wrote over four hundred poems, she accepted a Fulbright Scholarship at Cambridge University, England.

However, Plath's personal life was riddled with tragedy. Her father died when she was eight, and she suffered from bouts of depression that often rendered her suicidal. Indeed, Plath's early attempt to kill herself with sleeping pills provided the basis for her novel, *The Bell Jar* (1963). In 1956, Plath married the English poet Ted Hughes, and published her first book of poetry, *The Colossus*, four years later.

The poems in *The Colossus* only hint at the brilliance demonstrated in Plath's subsequent anthologies, such as *Ariel* (1965). Renowned for her combination of violent imagery and playful rhyme, Plath's poetry tackles her obsession with death and the wariness of life. But despite Plath's literary success, she was plagued by mental, financial, and personal troubles, including her separation from Hughes in 1962. A month after the publication of *The Bell Jar*, she took her own life by gassing herself in her London apartment.

Though Plath, the "feminist martyr" and "tragic victim," has been increasingly mythologized due to the nature of her death, the merit of her work has made her one of the most important female poets since 1900, and, in 1982, she became the first poet to win the Pulitzer Prize posthumously.

MARGARET ATWOOD

NOVEMBER 18, 1939

CANADIAN

Margaret Atwood is best known for her novel exploring themes such as gender and identity, *The Handmaid's Tale*, which was nominated for a number of awards and won the Arthur C. Clarke Award in 1986. It has found its way onto school, college, and university courses throughout the world, making Atwood's influence one that has extended generations and cultures.

Margaret Atwood's first novel, *The Edible Women* (1969), explores the construction of women's identity, through their body image, linked here to women's relationship with food, and the female body as fit for consumption in a phallocentric society. She followed this with *Surfacing* (1972) and *Lady Oracle* (1976), both widely recognized as among the most important feminist fictions of their day.

In *Lady Oracle*, the protagonist, Joan, is a fat woman and a writer of Gothic romances, who sees herself, through the eyes of the people around her, as a "female monster." The alienation of the female body, and the recognition that the construction of femininity is capable of change is an important motif in this and all Atwood's work. *Bodily Harm* (1981) focuses on women's role as victim of male aggression and a woman's body as a site of sexual exchange. The novel explores women's role in pornography and male violence.

However, *The Handmaid's Tale* (1985) still resonates as her most politically motivated novel. Atwood draws on the growing moral conservatism in North America and increasing fears of its influence on social and political life. The story is a terrifying portrayal of a religious state where life is wholly regulated, and it is one of the foremost feminist dystopias, a highly political novel that presents a future where women's hard-won freedoms are overturned. Brought to new fame through the 2017 American television series adaptation, Margaret Atwood's dystopian novel has taken on a further level of influence and meaning, to another generation of readers and watchers, placing her as one of the greatest dystopian writers in history.

Atwood's later novels include *Cat's Eye* (1988), the story of a woman painter, *The Robber Bride* (1993), *Alias Grace* (1996), about a young girl who murdered her employer, and *The Blind Assassin* (2000), whose protagonist, Iris, is 82 years old, and which won the 2000 Booker Prize. She continues to produce highly inventive, political novels, including the memorable *Oryx and Crake* (2003).

TRACEY EMIN

JULY 3, 1963

ENGLISH

Tracy Emin is a leading contemporary artist, best known for her work, *My Bed*. In 1999, it was exhibited at Tate Britain where Emin had been shortlisted for the Turner Prize. Like most of her work, it provoked widespread criticism and debate in the media, yet established her at the time as one of the best known of the "Young British Artists."

In the early 1990s, Emin sent letters to various people, offering them bonds for investment in her art. Jay Jopling responded by offering Emin her first solo show, *My Major Retrospective*, at Jay Jopling/ White Cube, London. That same year, Sarah Lucas, a prominent "Young British Artist" (YBA), hired Emin to help her run The Shop on Bethnal Green Road. Then, the following year, Emin set out with Carl Freedman on the tour across the U.S.

Emin gave readings from her autobiographical books, *Exploration of the Soul*, to help pay for the trip, and was photographed under a clear blue sky as she perched on a vintage chair in the desert. Across the upholstery, Emin had hand-stitched lettering and appliqué with the words "There's A lot of Money in Chairs." Emin dedicated the chair to her grandmother, who had given her this wise advice.

Returning to London, Emin opened Tracey Emin Museum within *Waterloo Road* (1995–98). In 1997, her tent *Everyone I Have Ever Slept With 1963–95*, also known as *The Tent*, was exhibited in *Sensation* at the Royal Academy of Arts as part of Charles Saatchi's YBA collection. In 1999, Emin was shortlisted for the Turner Prize, where she exhibited *My Bed*.

Now a prominent artist and celebrity, Emin would become as reputed for drunken outbursts on live network television, for instance, as for her art. Pieces like *The Tent* and *My Bed* were sparking controversy on a grand scale. However, even critics would describe Emin's work as "full of passion and striving and liveliness." It has also been called "emotional realism" and "thinking with the body."

❦

J. K. ROWLING

JULY 31, 1965

BRITISH

Responsible for creating one of the most famous characters in literary history, J. K. Rowling's Harry Potter is the orphan boy who discovers he is a wizard – and who has allegedly made his creator the richest and one of the most famous writers in history.

In a much-repeated anecdote, Harry Potter first appeared to J. K. Rowling in 1990, on a train journey from Manchester to London. She recalls: "I had never been so excited about an idea before... all the details bubbled up in my brain, and this scrawny, black-haired, bespectacled boy who didn't know he was a wizard became more and more real to me." She went on to plan the seven novels that would follow Harry through each of his seven years at Hogwarts School of Witchcraft and Wizardry – and then introduced him to the world in 1997.

Since then, as the star of a global publishing phenomenon and multi-million-pound merchandizing industry, Harry has sold upwards of 300 million novels and been credited with getting the children of the electronic age reading for pleasure again.

However, despite the fact that Harry champions ideals of courage, love, and loyalty, certain religious factions have condemned the books for their representations of witchcraft. Yet, J. K. Rowling is proud of the fact that her work appears yearly on international lists of most banned books, ironically putting her in the company of great writers such as Harper Lee and J. D. Salinger.

Since becoming the world's first billionaire author (and later relinquishing that status by giving most of her earnings to charity), she continues to have success as a crime writer under the pen name of Robert Galbraith, and through the popular Harry Potter screenplay, *Harry Potter and the Cursed Child* and movie spin off *Fantastic Beasts.*